OUR DYNAMIC WORLD: T

Ordinary Level Students use **TWO** textbooks:	Higher Level Stude
✸ *Our Dynamic World 1* (plus optional workbook)	✸ *Our Dynamic World 1* (plus optional w...
✸ *Our Dynamic World 2* **or** *Our Dynamic World 3*	✸ *Our Dynamic World 2* **or** *Our Dynamic World 3*
	✸ *Our Dynamic World 4* **or** *Our Dynamic World 5*

CORE
All students must cover Book 1 (Workbook highly recommended)

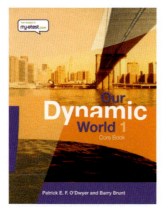

Book 1: covers the core sections of the syllabus which must be taken by all students

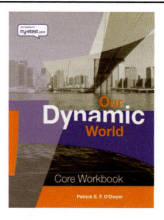

A workbook to accompany *Our Dynamic World 1*

ELECTIVES
All students must cover *either* Book 2 *or* Book 3

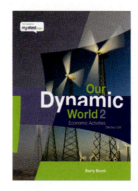 

Book 2: Economic Activities – Elective Unit

Book 3: The Human Environment – Elective Unit

OPTIONS
Higher Level only students cover *either* Book 4 *or* Book 5

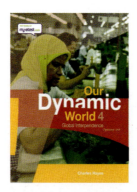 **Higher level only**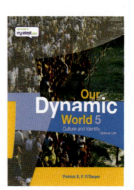

Book 4: Global Interdependence – Optional Unit

Book 5: Culture and Identity – Optional Unit

OUR DYNAMIC WORLD - THE SERIES

Ordinary Level Students use TWO textbooks:
- Our Dynamic World 1 (plus optional workbook)
- Our Dynamic World 2 or Our Dynamic World 3

Higher Level Students use THREE textbooks:
- Our Dynamic World 1 (plus optional workbook)
- Our Dynamic World 2 or Our Dynamic World 3
- Our Dynamic World 4 or Our Dynamic World 5

Book 1 - covers the core sections of the syllabus which must be taken by all students

A workbook to accompany Our Dynamic World 1

Book 2: Economic Activities - Elective Unit

Book 3: The Human Environment - Elective Unit

Higher Level only

Book 4: Global Interdependence - Optional Unit

Book 5: Culture and Identity - Optional Unit

Our Dynamic World

The Human Environment (Elective)

Patrick O'Dwyer

> **My-etest**
> Packed full of extra questions, **my-etest** lets you revise –
> at your own pace – when you want – where you want.
> Test yourself on our FREE website www.my-etest.com and check
> out how well you score!
> **Teachers!**
> Print an etest and give it for homework or a class test.

GILL & MACMILLAN

Gill & Macmillan Ltd
Hume Avenue
Park West
Dublin 12
with associated companies throughout the world
www.gillmacmillan.ie

© Patrick O'Dwyer 2004
0 7171 3520 9
Design, colour illustrations and print origination in Ireland by Design Image, Dublin
Colour reproduction by Ultragraphics, Dublin

The paper used in this book is made from the wood pulp of managed forests. For every tree felled, at least one tree is planted, thereby renewing natural resources.

All rights reserved.
No part of this publication may be copied, reproduced or transmitted in any form or by any means without written permission of the publishers or else under the terms of any licence permitting limited copying issued by the Irish Copyright Licensing Agency, 25 Denzille Lane, Dublin 2.

Acknowledgments
'Irish Attitudes to Refugees' © Patricia Casey

ELECTIVE UNIT: PATTERNS AND PROCESSES IN THE HUMAN ENVIRONMENT

	Content description	National settings	International settings
1	**The dynamics of population** Statement: **Population characteristics change over time and space (chapters 1–4)** Students should study changes in • population distribution • population density • growth patterns • population structure, changing fertility, and mortality rates.	Census material to show patterns of change in Ireland	Appropriate European and global examples
2	Statement: **Population characteristics have an impact on levels of human development (chapter 5)** Students should study the causes and effects of over-population, paying particular attention to • the impact of the development of resources • the influence of society and culture • the impact of income levels • the impact of technology on population growth Students should study the impact of growth rates on development.		Appropriate case studies
3	Statement: **Population movements have an impact on the donor and receiver regions (chapters 6–8)** Students should study • changing migration patterns in Ireland • migration policy in Ireland and the EU • ethnic, racial and religious issues which arise from migration • contrasting impacts of rural/urban migration in the developed and developing regions.	20th-century Irish census. Post-1950 migration to/from Ireland Government policy Growth in Irish cities	Appropriate examples

ELECTIVE UNIT: PATTERNS AND PROCESSES IN THE HUMAN ENVIRONMENT (continued)

	Content description	National settings	International settings
4	**The dynamics of settlement** Statement: **Settlements can be identified in relation to site, situation and function (chapters 9–14)** Students should study the locational characteristics for • pre-historic and historic settlements • rural settlement: including dispersed, clustered rural settlement and ribbon development • planning strategies in rural areas • site characteristics of urban settlements: an examination of hierarchy, hinterland and central place theory • how the functions and services of urban centres can change over time.	Historic development of Irish towns. National examples County and National Development Plan Appropriate Irish towns and cities	
5	Statement: **Urban settlements display an ever changing land use pattern and pose planning problems (chapters 15–17)** Students should study • land use zones within the modern city • changes in land use and planning issues, to include movement in industrial, residential and commercial land use • land values in cities and social stratification within cities • the expansion of cities and pressures on rural land use.	An Irish city	Appropriate world cities
6	Statement: **Problems can develop from the growth of urban centres (chapters 18–24)** Students should study • urban problems of traffic movement and congestion • urban decay and urban sprawl and the absence of community • heritage issues in urban areas • environmental quality • the effectiveness of urban planning strategies and urban renewal in solving urban problems • the expansion and problems in developing world cities • the future of urbanism. Issues related to the cities of the future.	Appropriate examples from Irish towns and cities Strategic urban plans	Case studies from developed world cities Case studies from developing world cities

Contents

Introduction		ix
Acknowledgments		x

Section 1	The Dynamics of Population	
Chapter 1	World Population Distribution	2
Chapter 2	World Population Density	5
Chapter 3	Past and Present Patterns in the Growth of Population	8
Chapter 4	Changing Population Characteristics	13

Section 2	Causes and Effects of Overpopulation	
Chapter 5	Overpopulation	26

Section 3	Migration	
Chapter 6	Changing Migration Patterns	38
Chapter 7	Ethnic, Racial and Religious Issues Created by Migration	49
Chapter 8	Rural to Urban Migration in the Developed and Developing World	56

Section 4	The Dynamics of Settlement	
Chapter 9	Site Characteristics of Villages, Towns and Cities	64
Chapter 10	Locational Characteristics of Ireland's Prehistoric and Historic Settlements	68
Chapter 11	Rural Settlement Patterns	86
Chapter 12	Planning Strategies in Rural Areas	89
Chapter 13	Urban Hierarchy, Hinterland and Central Place Theory	93
Chapter 14	The Functions and Services of Settlements Change Over Time	100

Section 5	Urban Land Use and Expansion	
Chapter 15	Changing Urban Land Use Patterns	106
Chapter 16	The Expansion of Cities and Pressure on Rural Land Use	113
Chapter 17	Residential Areas and Segregation Within Cities	116

Section 6	Urban Problems and Planning Strategies	
Chapter 18	Urban Problems in the Developed World	120
Chapter 19	Urban Decay, Urban Sprawl and the Absence of Community	127
Chapter 20	Conservation of the Built Environment	133
Chapter 21	Urban Growth and the Environment	134
Chapter 22	Urban Planning and Urban Renewal in Irish Cities	138
Chapter 23	Expansion and Problems in Developing World Cities	146
Chapter 24	The Future of Urbanism	153

Picture Credits	158

Introduction

This book covers Elective Unit 5 of the syllabus – Patterns and Processes in the Human Environment. It examines the dynamic nature of population: how it is always changing and never static, and how these changes affect the pattern and distribution of settlement. Settlements are also dynamic and as their functions, land uses and boundaries change over time, problems may develop that affect their living environments.

Case studies are used where possible to provide links between your core textbook, *Our Dynamic World 1*. This helps to tie the various sections of your course together and at the same time help to reduce the course content as much as possible, as directed by the syllabus.

The use of photographs and maps for class-based activities is an integral part of the syllabus. They will also form an equally important part of the Leaving Certificate Geography examination, so many map extracts and aerial photographs are used in relevant sections of this text to prepare students for their final exams.

Acknowledgments

The author wishes to thank the following people for their help and advice during the production of this script. Special thanks are due to Hubert Mahony, educational publishing director, for his constant expert advice and support. Thanks also due to managing editor Tess Tattersall, editor Jane Rogers, picture researcher Helen Thompson and the staff at Gill & Macmillan for their tireless work behind the scenes.

Sincere thanks to:
Dara O'Doherty and her team at Design Image for their creative and elegant design of this book; the Department of Geography at Maynooth university for sources of information on various topics in this text.

Pat O'Dwyer

SECTION 1 (CHAPTERS 1–4)
THE DYNAMICS OF POPULATION

 **KEY IDEA!** Population distribution, density, growth rates and structure change over time throughout the world.

This section explains how the distribution, density and growth patterns of the world's population have changed over time. It explains the reasons why many people live in some regions and why they tend to avoid or migrate from other areas.

Census material is used to examine changes in the structure, fertility and mortality rates of Ireland, while case studies of regions such as Japan and India in Asia and the Mezzogiorno in Italy are used as global and European examples for the same purpose.

Where possible, reference is made to regions studied in the regional section of your core text book, *Our Dynamic World 1*, as part of the 'settings' requirements of the new syllabus. This pattern is continued throughout the textbook.

- Chapter 1   World Population Distribution
- Chapter 2   World Population Density
- Chapter 3   Past and Present Patterns in the Growth of Population
- Chapter 4   Changing Population Characteristics

Some regions, such as deserts, have low population densities

Urban regions are areas of high population density

Due to improved technology, people in advanced societies have a long life expectancy

CHAPTER 1
WORLD POPULATION DISTRIBUTION

> In each case give one fully developed reason why there are so few people in regions A and B. Use your atlas to help you.

Because the distribution, density and number of people in the world is never static it is said to be **dynamic**. It is constantly changing over time and over the earth's surface.

Population numbers vary throughout the world and between continents. They also vary between countries, within countries and within local areas, such as counties. These variations happened in the past and continue to occur today.

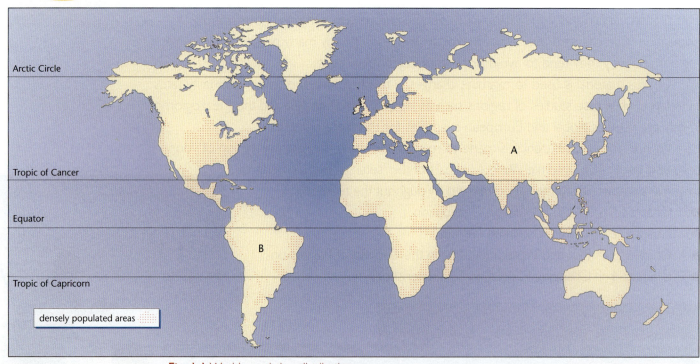

Fig. 1.1 World population distribution

> World population distribution means the location and number of people who live in each continent.

The world's population is very unevenly distributed. However, there are **four distinct areas** where most of the world's population is located:
- West and central Europe.
- The eastern United States and south-eastern Canada.
- The Indian sub-continent including Pakistan, India, Sri Lanka and Bangladesh.
- East and south-east Asia including China, Korea, Japan, Malaysia, the Philippines and Indonesia.

These areas are all in the **northern hemisphere** and lie mostly in **temperate** or **sub-tropical** latitudes. Outside these main areas of concentration people are much more thinly spread. However, there are small pockets of large numbers of people in places such as Egypt, Java, south-east Brazil and California.

There are many areas, often of great size, which are very **thinly populated**. These are usually areas that are inaccessible, are mountainous or too cold, too hot, too wet or too dry. These areas include:

- The **cold tundra** and ice cap regions of polar lands, e.g. Northern Canada, Greenland, Siberia and Antarctica.
- **Mountainous lands,** e.g. the Himalayas, plateau lands of central Asia, such as Tibet, and the Rocky Mountains in the USA and Canada.
- **Hot deserts** such as the Sahara, the Arabian and the Australian deserts.
- **Equatorial rainforests**, such as the Amazon, Borneo and the Congo.

People generally avoid such hot barren areas

Population distribution maps are an inaccurate way of representing population distribution. For example, in India, even though it has a very high population (over 1 billion people at present), many parts of the country are sparsely populated while other areas are overpopulated. A better measure represents the ratio of people in a country per unit of area of agriculturally productive land. This is called the **physiologic density**. In India this index is about 650 per square kilometre (about 1600 per square mile).

Water and food are two essential needs of people for survival. So it is no accident that the great lowlands, which are reasonably level and usually have deep, fertile soils such as river flood plains, are mostly areas of high population. High, rugged, mountainous areas with their thin, stony soils and cold, windy climates have low population numbers. However, owing to climactic change or other factors, some places that had large populations at one time are now thinly populated, and places that were once thinly peopled are now heavily populated.

> Today, over half the world's population lives in India, China and south-east Asia

Class activity

1. Write a brief note about how each of the following factors may affect population distribution:
   - Accessibility
   - Water supply
   - Relief
   - Mineral deposits
   - Climate
   - Natural vegetation
   - Soil fertility

2. Identify the regions of high population density in each of the following continents:
   (a) North America; (b) South America;
   (c) Europe; (d) Asia.

3. Name three regions of the world with a very low population.

4. For each region named in question 3 above, explain one reason why it has a low population.

THE DYNAMICS OF POPULATION

Fig. 1.2 Distribution of world cities with populations of over 1 million

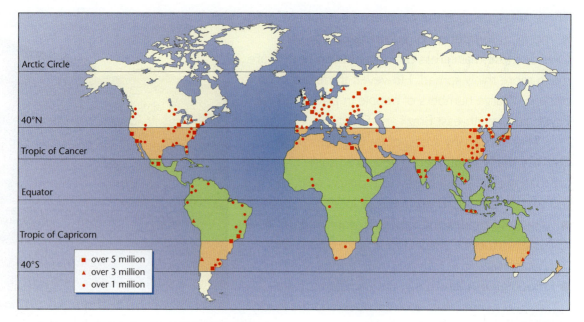

Fig. 1.3 Urban population growth. The increased urbanisation of the world's population has created changes in its distribution over time.

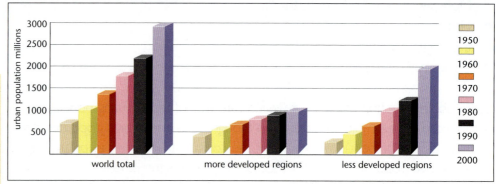

Class activity
Carefully examine the distribution map of world cities of one million or more people, Figure 1.2, and the bar graph of urban population growth, Figure 1.3.
1. Identify an overall pattern of location for most of these large cities.
2. Which continent at present has the largest number of cities with a population in excess of 5 million people?
3. Which continent has the least number? Explain why.
4. Identify and explain the pattern in the distribution of cities in the developed world and the developing world.
5. What overall pattern/s of urban growth is/are evident from your study of Figure 1.3?

THE EFFECTS OF URBANISATION ON WORLD POPULATION DISTRIBUTION

The **growth of towns and cities**, and industrialisation, have changed the pattern of world population over the past 200 years and especially during the twentieth century. Large-scale migration of rural residents to towns and cities takes place as a country develops from an agricultural to an industrial economy. During this process, the growth rate of urban areas is typically double the pace of overall population increase. Some 29 per cent of the world population was living in urban areas in 1950. This figure was 43 per cent in 1990 and 50 per cent in 2000.

Urbanisation eventually leads to a **severe decline in the number of people living in the countryside** with **negative population growth rates**. Cities are engines of social change; they continue to grow throughout the developing world. In 1960, one in three people lived in a city; today half of all people do, and **it is predicted that by 2030 more than 60 per cent of the population will live in urban areas**. More and more of these will be megacities with more than 10 million people. The number of such cities has grown from two in 1960 to 17 today, and is projected to reach 26 by 2015: 22 in less-developed regions; 18 in Asia. All of these megacities lie within 500 kilometres of a coastline.

CHAPTER 2
WORLD POPULATION DENSITY

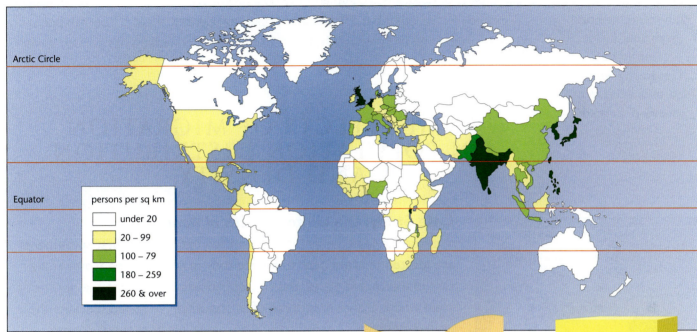

Fig. 2.1 World population density

For most people:
- One-fifth of the earth is too cold.
- One-fifth of the earth is too hot.
- One-fifth of the earth is too wet.
- One-fifth of the earth is too dry.

So most of the world's people live on one-fifth of the world's surface, which is scattered throughout the various continents.

World population **distribution** means the location and number of people who live in each continent. Population **density** means the average number of people per square kilometre in a country.

To obtain population densities, divide the total population of a country by the total area of that country. The densities are then grouped into categories, and each category is given a lighter or darker colour on a map to represent a lower or a higher density respectively. While these maps are simple to understand they often hide the irregularities of population within some countries.

HOW POPULATION DENSITY VARIES THROUGHOUT THE WORLD

The map in Figure 2.1 displays population densities throughout the world at present. It clearly shows that the greatest densities occur in south and south-east Asia, where over half of the world's population lives.

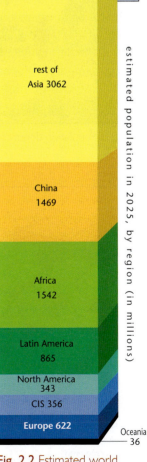

Fig. 2.2 Estimated world population in 2025, by region (in millions)

THE DYNAMICS OF POPULATION

A closer examination of these densities would indicate that the statistics hide irregularities. For example, India is shown with a density of at least 260 people per square kilometre. However, few people live in the Thar Desert in northern India or in the higher parts of the Deccan Plateau, while densities of over 2,000 per hectare may occur in parts of Kolkata (Calcutta) and Mumbai (Bombay).

Ireland, on the other hand, has a low population density of just 57 people per square kilometre. Yet Dublin has a higher density, while Connemara has a much lower population density.

> Can you remember from your Junior Certificate Geography which part of Brazil is most densely populated? Why?

SOME EFFECTS OF MIGRATION ON POPULATION DISTRIBUTION AND DENSITY

Fig. 2.3 Population density in the USA

Case Study: the United States of America

In junior certificate geography you studied that peoples' **first settlements are located in areas near to where they originally came from**. In the case of the United States, this concept applies especially to the north-east coast where a large proportion of its population is located. Because the north-east coast is nearest to Europe, emigrants from the European continent settled here. Over time this has led to a high population density in this area. The concentration of large cities, such as Washington D.C., Pittsburgh, New York, Albany and Boston, as well as numerous other cities and towns, forms a large urban region called a **megalopolis**.

There is a much lower population density in the mid-west (the Mississippi basin) as it is away from the coast and is separated from it by the Appalachian mountain range, which initially formed a physical barrier to westward migration of new settlers.

Case Study: southern Italy

Migration, especially up to the 1970s, was a major factor in accounting for differences in population densities within Italy. Besides the norm of rural to urban migration, the migration of people from southern Italy (the Mezzogiorno) to northern Italy has led to a pattern of out-migration in the south and a corresponding pattern of in-migration in the north.

Over 4 million people left the Mezzogiorno between 1951 and 1971, and over 1.1 million people left between 1983 and 1993. Today, due to new investments in the region as a consequence of the Mezzogiorno being classed as Objective 1 status, employment prospects have been improved and out-migration is lower than before. However, out-migration still continues because growth in job prospects has failed to satisfy demands.

Fig. 2.4 Population density in Italy
A North West
B North East Centre
C Mezzogiorno

WORLD POPULATION DENSITY

You studied in your Junior Certificate course that migration (for various reasons) has led to changes in population distribution and population density in many parts of the world, such as Ulster, the West of Ireland and Brazil.

Today, international migration is becoming an **important political issue** on all regions. Numbers of migrants are increasing and the issues raised by migration become more important. Between 1965 and 1990, migration grew from 75 million to 120 million people world-wide.

A hill-top village in the Mezzogiorno. *Identify some characteristics of this village that suggest it is poor.*

Class activity
Study Figure 2.1 on page 5.
1. Name the countries with a population density of 260 and over persons per square kilometre.
2. With the aid of your atlas, explain why Australia and Canada have such low population densities.

Class activity
Carefully study the population density distribution map of Italy (Fig. 2.4) on the previous page.
1. Which region of Italy has the lowest density of population?
2. Which region has the highest density?
3. With the help of your atlas and your studies in *Our Dynamic World 1*, explain:
   (a) why south-eastern Italy has a greater density of population than most other parts of the Mezzogiorno;
   (b) why the area around Naples has a high density population.

Do you remember from Our Dynamic World 1 what Objective 1 status means?

Class activity
Study Figure 1.1 on page 2. Explain the historical factors why
(a) the north-east coast of the United States has a large population;
(b) Mexico has a large population;
(c) many people have migrated from the Mezzogiorno.

TEST YOURSELF AT my-etest.com

CHAPTER 3
PAST AND PRESENT PATTERNS IN THE GROWTH OF POPULATION

It is estimated that the population of the world in 9000 B.C. was about 10 million. At this time people wandered from place to place in search of wild cereals. Then people in Mesopotamia (the valleys of the Tigris and Euphrates in Iraq) discovered that by using seeds from wild cereals and scattering them on fertile ground they would grow, flourish and produce crops for food. This eliminated their need to wander and so they became the first farmers, and the first urban dwellers. The discovery and spread of agriculture led to a speeding up of population growth. Initially population growth was slow. When Christ was born there were about 260 million people on earth. Growth rates continued to fluctuate because of wars, famines, persecution, disease and natural disasters. It took nearly 1700 years for the world's population to reach 800 million people.

Then suddenly, after 1750, the population began to grow rapidly. This change came about because of:

- **New farming methods and improved technology.** New farming methods, such as the enclosure of land and the creation of farms, better breeds of animals and the use of new farm machines, such as the seed drill, led to a large increase in food production.
- **The invention of the steam engine.** This development led to employment for thousands of workers in coalfield areas in Europe. Improved income and the development of nearby terraced housing led to larger families and the growth of towns and cities.

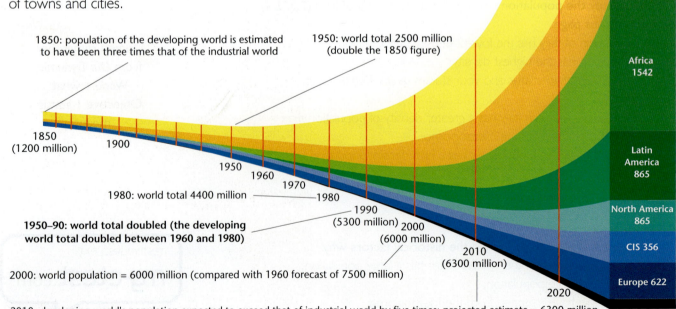

Fig. 3.1 World population growth

- **Improved hygiene and medical knowledge** allowed a longer and healthier life than ever before.
- **Increased land supply** due to the colonisation of lands in the New World.

GROWTH PATTERNS

All continents shared a five-fold population increase over a 300-year period – from about 500 million in 1650 to 2.5 billion in 1950 – but increases were most striking in advanced countries where new technologies were invented and applied.

Beginning about 1950, a **new phase** of population growth occurred when **famine and disease could be controlled**, when vaccines, antibiotics, insecticides and high-yielding varieties of seeds were introduced. With improvements in water supplies, sewage disposal facilities and transportation, agricultural yields increased, and deaths from infectious diseases greatly declined. Life expectancy at birth in most developing countries increased from about 35–40 years in 1950 to 61 years by 1990. The rapid decline in deaths among people who continued to have large families led to annual population growth in developing nations that doubles population size in 25 years or less.

> **Birth rate/death rate/natural increase**
> **Birth rate** refers to the number of births for every 1,000 people in a country for one year. The **natural increase** is found when the birth rate is measured against the number of deaths (death rate) for every 1,000 people in the same year.

> Population change may differ from the natural increase or decrease because it also takes into account migrants that include emigrants (out) and immigrants (in).

What statistics fail to show is the great variation in population growth between different areas in the world and especially between economically developed and economically developing continents. To achieve a stable world population the average family of today would, world-wide, have to have 2.3 children. At present, while the average number for Europe and Russia, North America and, due to political influence, China is under two, it is over four in most of Asia and Latin America and over six in Africa (see Figure 3.1).

Vital to any assessment of a region's social and economic status is the rate of its **natural increase**. In south-east Asia, for example, many countries have growth rates of 2.0 per cent per year. When populations grow this fast it is difficult to improve living standards. The needs of the newly born absorb most of the gains. Muslim countries tend to have high growth rates and so short doubling times. Take Pakistan, whose present population is 150 million people. The latest figures show its rate of natural increase as 2.8 per cent and its doubling

> **Where is Latin America?**
> Latin America includes Mexico and all countries south of it to the southern tip of South America.

Identify two factors that encourage large families in some countries

THE DYNAMICS OF POPULATION

time 25 years. So at present rates Pakistan will have 300 million people by 2027. India will have 2 billion people by 2040 (remember there were only 3.5 billion people in the entire world just 25 years ago).

Natural increase in a population occurs when the **birth rate is greater than the death rate**. When the death rate is greater than the birth rate there is a **natural decrease**.

Case Studies: Change Over Time
Past and present population trends for Britain

Remember from your Junior Certificate the Demographic Model ... the **population cycle** as illustrated here by Britain. Demography means the study of population.

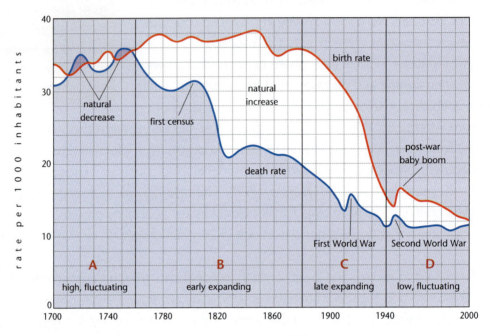

Fig. 3.2 Changes in Britain's population, 1700–2002

Britain was the world's first industrialised country. Based on their home supplies of coal and iron ore, the Scottish, Welsh and English coalfield areas became quickly industrialised. Within a fifty-year period, 1750–1800, coal-mining villages became towns and towns became cities. Increased incomes from industrial work and improvements in medical knowledge led to lower death rates and high population increases.

Class activity
1. Identify and explain four factors that caused world population to rise rapidly since 1750.
2. Explain how population rates in a few regions of the world may dramatically affect world population numbers.

PAST AND PRESENT PATTERNS IN THE GROWTH OF POPULATION

> **Class activity**
> Carefully examine the population model for Britain, Figure 3.2.
> 1. Explain why Britain had high birth and death rates prior to 1760.
> 2. What factors caused the rapid fall in death rates between 1760 and 1940?
> 3. Explain why there has been a levelling off of birth and death rates with slight fluctuations since 1940.
> 4. Suggest what trend may occur in Britain's population between 2000 and 2010.
> 5. What effects had the First and Second World Wars on Britain's (a) birth rates and (b) death rates?
> 6. Why is Britain's population growth an important one to compare to the demographic transition model? (Hint: first industrialised country.)

Regional Growth Patterns Over Time and Space

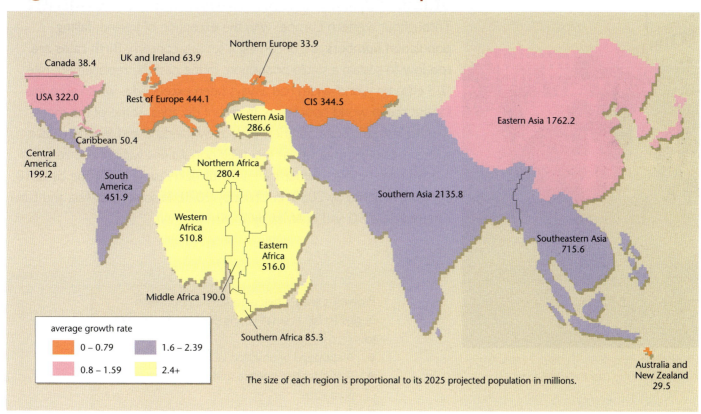

Fig. 3.3 Future population growth patterns

In 1990, 1.2 billion people lived in the developed nations of the world, and 4.1 billion people lived in the less developed countries. By region, over half the world's population was in east and south Asia: China, with more than 1.2 billion inhabitants, and India, with some 960 million, had the highest populations. Europe and the countries of the former USSR contained 15 per cent, North and South America made up 14 per cent, and Africa had 12 per cent of world population.

Differences in regional growth rates are altering these percentages over time. Africa's share of the world population is expected to more than double by the year 2025, while the populations of south Asia and Latin America remain nearly constant and the other regions, including east Asia, decline **in relative size**. The share of the present

11

developed nations in world population – 23 per cent in 1990 – is expected to fall to 17 per cent by 2025. Nine out of every 10 persons who are now being added to the world's population are living in the less developed countries.

Class activity
Carefully study the chart of future growth patterns on page 11.
1. Which region of the world has the greatest population?
2. Which region has the smallest population?
3. Does the answer to question 2 mean that natural increase in this region has been the least when compared to other more populated regions? Explain fully.
4. Explain the meaning of the term 'relative size' in the text.

China's one-child policy has kept its population in check over the past three decades

Stable Populations in Industrialised Countries

Throughout western Europe, with the exception of Ireland, **falling population numbers** are becoming a serious concern. **Birth rates are too low** to sustain a stable population. In the past the replacement rate (2.3 children world-wide) had always been exceeded – which accounts for the rise in world population. In recent decades, some of the more wealthy industrialised countries, such as Switzerland and Sweden, have such small young populations that their populations will achieve zero growth rates (stable, neither increasing or decreasing) in Europe by 2010, in North America by 2030, in China by 2070, in south-east Asia and Latin America by 2090 and in Africa by 2100.

Problems arise when a country's population begins to fall. A small young population can lead to:
- A shortage of unskilled labour.
- A shortage of science and technology graduates.
- A shortage of taxes to sustain pensions and services.

Debate this issue or China's one-child policy in class. Trocaire has a video on this topic: maybe you could get this and look at it in class.

Class activity
Explain how a rapid fall in Ireland's birth rate might affect
(a) schools;
(b) subsidies for old-age pensioners;
(c) the attraction of foreign industry to Ireland.

CHAPTER 4
CHANGING POPULATION CHARACTERISTICS

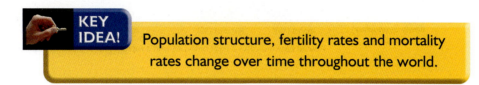

KEY IDEA! Population structure, fertility rates and mortality rates change over time throughout the world.

Three important basic characteristics of a population are its:
- **Age structure**, which refers to the proportions of a population that belong to different age groups.
- **Sex structure** refers to the ratio between the number of males and females.
- **Dependency ratio** refers to the number of people who are **economically inactive**, children and old age pensioners compared to those who are **economically active** (the working population) and on whom they depend to support them.

AGE–SEX STRUCTURE

The best way to illustrate the population structure and future trends is by an **age-sex pyramid**. In your junior certificate you studied these pyramids for Brazil and Germany. These pyramids usually divide the population into **5-year age** groups, 0–4, 5–9, 10–14 and so on. As there are generally more young people than old the diagram has the general shape of a pyramid. The differences in age, sex, birth rates and death rates create an irregular shape that indicates the structure of a population.

As well as showing **past changes** they can predict short and long-term **future changes** or **trends** in population. Age-sex pyramids are regularly used by governments to forecast future **social needs** such as the number of schools, teachers, hospitals or hospital extensions or community care nurses needed in any given area. These statistics can be applied to both **national** and **regional** levels, such as counties and cities. For example, a narrow base indicates that fewer schools and teachers will be needed. A wide top indicates more nursing homes may be needed. Population pyramids can show the effects of migration, the age and sex of migrants and the effects of large-scale wars, famines and epidemics or disease.

The population pyramids of individual countries vary greatly in the details of their shape. But population pyramids can be reduced to four basic types. These basic models are not 'written in stone', as each pyramid will differ from the next, but they are a useful guide to the study of populations. Examples of four pyramids have been chosen (Figures 4.1 and 4.3 on the following pages) because they correspond closely with the model.

THE DYNAMICS OF POPULATION

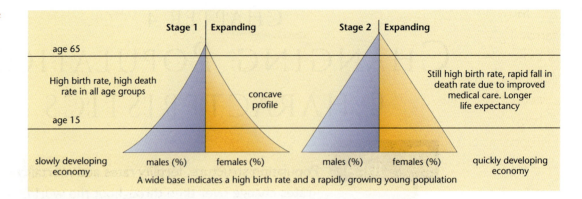

Fig. 4.1 Fewer children die as an economy develops

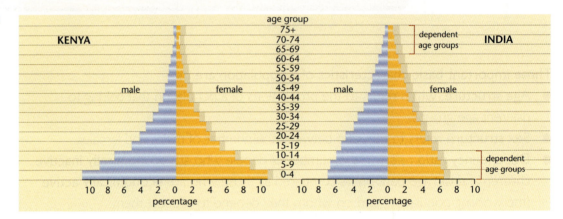

Fig. 4.2 Population pyramids of Kenya and India

Class activity

Carefully study the population pyramids of Kenya and India in Figure 4.2. For both Kenya and India:
1. Calculate the total percentage (male and female) aged between 0 and 14 years.
2. Calculate the total percentage (male and female) aged 65+.
3. From your calculations state which country has (a) the highest percentage of children; (b) the highest percentage of old people.
4. From your study of the population cycle, explain the reasons for the percentages in 3(a) and (b) above.
5. Which of these two countries could best afford free: (a) primary education; (b) secondary education; (c) third-level education? Explain each of your answers fully.
6. Which pyramid shape indicates (a) an industrially emergent country; (b) a newly industrialised country? Explain.

SEX STRUCTURE

Having a **balance** of males versus females in a population is **important**. For instance, a sex ratio of fewer than 90 or more than 110 males for every 100 females is regarded as distinctly unbalanced. This may relate to a particular area of a country such as the West of Ireland or to total population.

Sex ratio can vary within different age groups. For example, there are more baby boys than baby girls. Infant mortality rates are higher among boys, as are death rates in most or all age groups for males. By old age, there are generally more females than males as women have a longer life expectancy.

Irregularities in a population pyramid may exist for a number of reasons, such as a narrowing in the young adult group. This may result from **out-migration**, or **war** (many of those killed being males). If such a narrowing exists it will move up the pyramid as time passes, so that 25 years later it will be at the 50–60 years level. It could also reflect a reduced birth rate that may have lasted only a few years before increasing again. A 'baby boom', such as that which followed the ending of the Second World War, has the opposite effect, creating a temporary bulge in the pyramid, that also moves up the pyramid with time (see Figure 4.5, page 17).

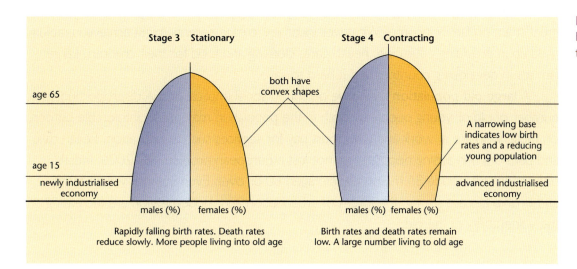

Fig. 4.3 As a country becomes richer, many live to old age

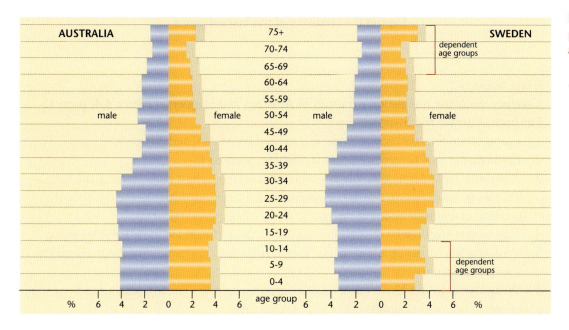

Fig. 4.4 Population pyramids of Australia and Sweden

Class activity
The pyramids for Australia and Sweden represent economically advanced nations.
(a) Explain why Australia is classed as at a stationary change.
(b) Explain why Sweden is classed as at a contracting stage.
(c) Explain reasons for the differences between both pyramids.
In your answer refer to (i) young dependent and (ii) old dependent age groups.

DEPENDENCY RATIO

One of the most important aspects of the age structure of a population is its dependency ratio.

A **large young population** represents a vast potential market for consumer goods. In the developing world, 36 per cent of the population is under 15. In recent years nothing has excited multi-national companies as much as the 'opening up' of China and other Asian markets in newly industrialised countries such as Thailand and South Korea. The attraction lies in the prospective buying power of these new customers.

A developing country generally has a large young population. Large families place a great strain on family income. Whatever income increase parents might achieve is rapidly used up in providing education, health care, clothing and food for their children. Large families in developing countries find it hard to save.

A **large old population** may have profound social implications. A disproportionate number of old or young people or both in the population may put an intolerable burden on those who are at work and who must pay for services such as education, health care and pensions. An ageing population is not just a European problem. By 2006, India's population will include 86 million people aged 60 or over. Even in India, where family and kinship ties are strong, the forces of urbanisation and modernisation are increasing the vulnerability of the old.

> Countries such as Sweden, with such a reduction in numbers of young people leading to a declining population, suggest that a fifth stage should be added to the population cycle: the senile stage.

Class activity
Explain the meaning of this last sentence.

Class activity
Carefully study the population pyramids of Australia and Sweden in Figure 4.4, page 15. For both Australia and Sweden:
1. Calculate the total percentage (male and female) between 0 and 14 years.
2. Calculate the total percentage (male and female) aged 65+.
3. From your calculations, state which country has: (a) the highest percentage of children; (b) the highest percentage of old people; (c) the highest percentage in the dependent groups; (d) the highest total in the economically active (working) group.
4. Suggest one reason why Australia has a small number of males in the 40–49 age group.
5. What characteristics in the pyramid of Sweden's population indicate that it has a declining young population?
6. What advantages/problems might Sweden experience in the coming decades as a consequence of its population structure? Explain fully.
7. Explain why Australia's age–sex pyramid is classed as stationary.

Case Study: Japan

The percentage of Japan's elderly population is getting increasingly larger. Its percentage of young people is getting increasingly smaller. This is creating a top-heavy population pyramid, which has serious implications for its economy. Japanese people are the most long-lived in the world. In 2000, there were more than 10,500 Japanese people (83 per cent of them female) over 100 years of age, 1,700 (16 per cent) more than in 1999. By 2025, nearly 26 per cent of the Japanese people will be aged 65 years or more, compared to just 12 per cent in 1990.

The cost of caring for such a large percentage of old people will be enormous, especially if its birth rate continues to decline. Women are being encouraged to bear more children, even though Japan's population density is one of the highest in the world, over 860 people per square kilometre. However, its physiologic population density is 7950 per square mile (3070 per square kilometre).

Physiologic density refers to the number of people in a country relative to the amount of productive agricultural land.

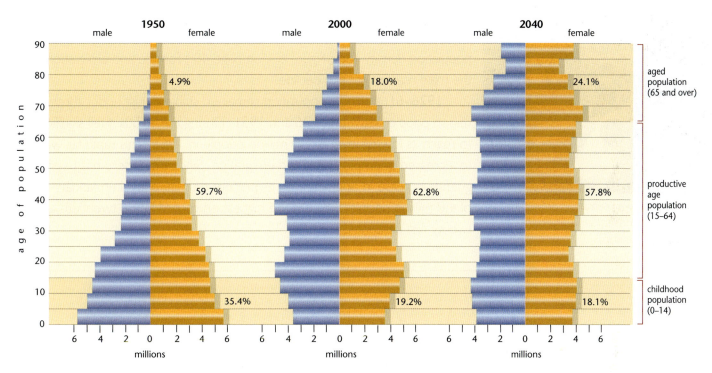

Fig. 4.5 Changes in the population structure of Japan over time

Class activity
Carefully study the population pyramids for Japan from 1950 to 2040 (Figure 4.5).
1. Compare and contrast the changes that have occurred in Japan's population from 1950 to 2000.
2. What (a) social and (b) economic forces have caused the changes displayed in these pyramids?
3. State the causes and consequences of projected changes to Japan's population structure from 2000 to 2040. In your answer, refer especially to dependency ratios of young and old people.
4. Into which, if any, of the four age–sex pyramid categories would you place Japan's pyramid of 2040? Explain your choice.

THE DYNAMICS OF POPULATION

Case study: patterns of population change in Ireland

KEY IDEA! Ireland's population declined from 1841 to 1961. It rose from 1961 to 2004.

Apart from Luxembourg, Ireland has the smallest population in western Europe. It also has the lowest population density: 51 persons per square kilometre.

The Republic of Ireland's population declined from just over 6.5 million people in 1841 to under 3.0 million by 1926. At that time the majority of Irish people lived in rural areas. The West of Ireland, especially, had a high population density. (See Figure 6.1 on page 40.) Famine and emigration were the main reasons for this decline.

1926–61. Ireland's population remained stable at just under three million people between 1926 and 1951. During the 1950s it fell significantly to reach its lowest level of 2.8 million people in 1961. This rapid fall was due to increased unemployment and emigration. Since then there has been a gradual increase in population to its present estimated level (in January 2004) of 4.0 million people, which is the highest on record in the twentieth and twenty-first centuries.

Ireland's young population is decreasing due to better education levels and higher living standards

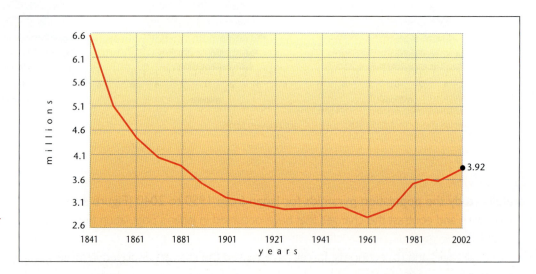

Fig. 4.6 Ireland's population for its 26 counties, 1841–2002

Between 1961 and 2002 the growth pattern in Ireland's population has been influenced by:
- Changing emigration patterns.
- Changing fertility rates.
- Improved economy.

Class activity
Carefully study the population graph for Ireland, Figure 4.6.
1. What was Ireland's population in 1841 and 1951?
2. Did Ireland's population rise or fall during this time?
3. What was the main reason for this change?
4. What was the pattern of change in Ireland's population between 1851 and 1961?
5. What was the main cause of this trend? Explain fully.
6. What was the population trend between 1961 and 2002? Suggest some reasons for this trend.

CHANGING POPULATION CHARACTERISTICS

KEY IDEA! Ireland's population structure, fertility rates and mortality rates have changed over time.

Age structure

There are clear changes in the age structure of Ireland's population since 1961.

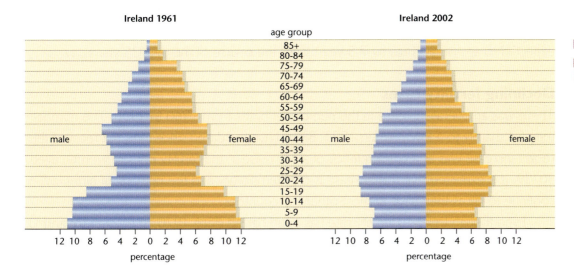

Fig. 4.7 Population pyramids of Ireland, 1961 and 2002

Class activity

Carefully study the age-sex pyramids for Ireland in 1961 and 2002, Figure 4.7.
Use evidence from these charts to support your answers to the following questions:
1. What characteristic dominates Ireland's age structure for 1961?
2. From what you have studied so far explain the main causes of this characteristic.
3. What has happened since then, and especially in recent years, to eliminate this feature?
4. Into which stage would you place Ireland's pyramid for (a) 1961 and (b) 2002? (See pages 14 and 5.)
5. How does Ireland's age structure differ between the two charts for the age groups 0–19, 40–59 and 80+?

Because emigration affects the young adult groups aged 15 to 39, their loss creates an imbalance between the various age groups. This is clearly seen in the age-sex pyramid, Figure 4.7, by a narrowing of the pyramid in the centre. The absence of those emigrants reduced the potential natural increase as it reduced the numbers of women of childbearing age in the population at that time.

A large population of old people demand increased levels of medical care

In the 2002 age-sex pyramid a narrowing of the base indicates fewer children and consequently an increasingly older population. This reduction in child numbers also reduces the number of potential women of childbearing age in the near future.

An ageing population

The age structure of the population at any time depends on past trends in fertility, mortality and migration. There has been a fall in the number of births since 1980. The average age of the population was 33.6 years in 1996 compared with 30.8 years in 1981. The population aged nearly three years in the 15-year period 1981–96 and it is expected to age on average by 7.5 years over the course of the next 35 years.

Declining fertility rates

There was an overall increase in the number of births from 1960 to 1980. The number then fell sharply to a low point in 1994. Births have increased since then but most of this recent increase was as a consequence of an increase in the fertility rates of women aged 30–39. It is expected that this increase is only temporary and the number of births will continue to fall as they have in most other EU countries.

Even though Ireland's fertility rate has been halved since 1970, at present **Ireland continues to have the highest fertility rate in the EU.**

> Can you remember the meaning of replacement level? It is the number of births that are needed to create a stable population – that is, a population that is neither increasing nor decreasing.

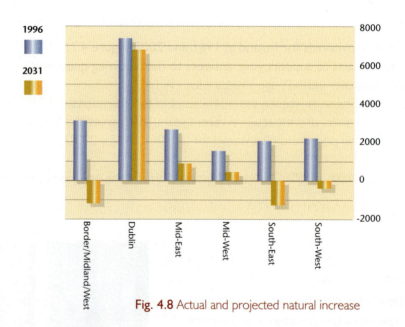

Fig. 4.8 Actual and projected natural increase

> Remember the New Regional Divisions of the country from your Regional Geography in *Our Dynamic World 1*.

Class activity

Carefully study the bar chart, Figure 4.8.
1. Which region has the highest natural increase, and why?
2. Which region has the lowest natural increase, and why?
3. How has Ireland's fertility rate changed since 1970?
4. Give reasons for this change.

The decline in birth rates came about mainly because of changing attitudes to women in Irish society. These changes include:
- Changing attitudes to family planning.
- Increasing numbers of women (both married and single) in the workforce.
- Increased educational achievements.

Mortality rates

Life expectancy at birth increased for men from 57.4 years in 1926 to 73 in 1996. This represents a gain of 15.6 years over the 70-year period. The corresponding female rates were 57.9 and 78.7 years respectively – a gain of 20.8 years. The major gains in both male and female life expectancy were recorded in the immediate post-war period, 1946–61. These gains resulted from improved living conditions as well as from advances in maternity services and medical treatment. These included immunisation, and the virtual elimination of tuberculosis (TB), which significantly increased survival rates. The reduction was most noticeable in the case of infant deaths.

Despite the improvements that have occurred, life expectancy for both males and females in Ireland remains relatively **low compared with many other EU countries**, see Table 4.1.

It is expected that female life expectancy will be **84 years** and male life expectancy **77.8 years in 2031**. Life expectancy in all EU countries is expected to continue to improve.

What evidence in this photograph indicates that elderly people are increasingly enjoying an active retirement?

Country	Males	Females
Austria	74.6	81.15
Belgium	74.6	81.4
Denmark	74.1	79.4
Finland	73.9	81.3
France	75.1	83.01
Germany	74.4	80.9
Greece	76.03	81.2
Iceland	77.3	81.9
Ireland	74.2	79.9
Italy	75.9	82.5
Luxembourg	74.02	80.8
Netherlands	75.5	81.4
Norway	75.8	81.9
Portugal	72.4	79.6
Spain	75.4	82.6
Sweden	77.07	82.5
Switzerland	76.8	82.7
United Kingdom	75.13	80.66

Table 4.1 Life expectancy in selected European countries

Class activity

Carefully study the figures for life expectancy in the European countries listed in Table 4.1.
1. Which country has the longest life expectancy for (a) females and (b) males?
2. Suggest why the longest life expectancy for males is not achieved in the same country as that for females.
3. What advantages do those countries with higher life expectancies have over other countries/regions?
4. Suggest why Ireland has such low life expectancies when compared with other countries.
5. Suggest reasons why life expectancy has improved in recent years.

THE DYNAMICS OF POPULATION

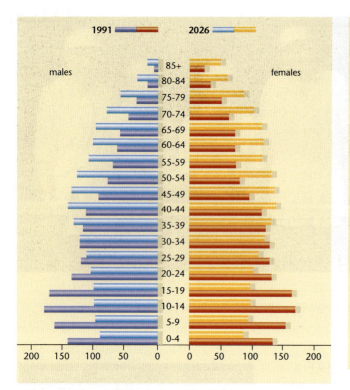

Fig. 4.9 Population pyramids for Ireland, 1991 and 2026

Class activity

Carefully study the population pyramids for 1991 and 2026 in Figure 4.9.

1. Identify the future fertility rate trend in the age groups 0 to 24. What effect will this trend have on the dependency ratio between now and 2026?
2. Identify the future trend in the age groups 60 to 85+. What effect will this trend have on the dependency ratio?
3. Explain fully how the combined population numbers in the age groups 25 to 59 (working ages) might cope with the needs of groups listed in questions 1 and 2 in 2026.
4. From your understanding of population pyramids so far explain the 'quality of life' one would expect to have in Ireland in 2026. Use evidence from the chart to support your answer.
5. Into which category would you classify Ireland's population pyramid for 2026? (See pyramid categories on pages 14 and 15.)

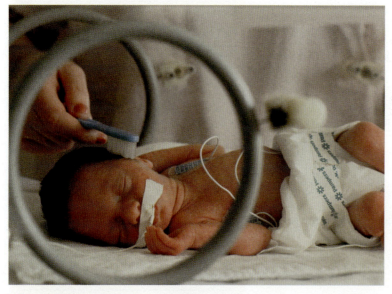

What advances in medical care ensure that mortality rates in Ireland continue to remain low?

Emigration had both positive and negative effects on the Irish economy prior to 1961.

Dependency ratio

Up to 1961. The main factors that influence the dependency ratio in Ireland are changes over time in birth rates, death rates and emigration/immigration. For that reason, Ireland's dependency ratio has changed sharply since 1961. In the age-sex pyramid for 1961 (Figure 4.7), it is clear there is a narrowing in the graph from ages 15 to 44. This means that there were few people of working age who supported a large number of children (a wide base caused by a high fertility rate) and a large number of pensioners (a wide top caused by a reducing death rate). This narrowing resulted from increased emigration during the 1950s of young adults, both male and female (but more males than females), seeking work abroad.

So there was a sharp rise in the dependency ratio during the 1950s as a consequence of migration.

Since 1980

There has been a **constant decline in the dependency ratio since 1980**. This is due to a fall in birth rates during this time (a narrowing of the base caused by reducing birth rates/fertility rates). There has also been a slight decrease in the age groups over 65 years of age. These reductions have caused a **bulge** in the working age groups (see Figure 4.7, page 19) and so have reduced the overall dependency ratio.

As time moves on some **other factors** will aid the dependency ratio:

- **Immigration** (in-migration). If inward migration continues as is expected (about 15,000 is predicted annually for 2001–2006), it will increase the percentage of people in working age groups and consequently will relieve some pressure from the ratio.
- **Working students**. The percentage of part-time working students is rising quickly. The rate for 15–19-year-olds grew from 4.5 per cent in 1996 to 11 per cent in 1998, while for 20–24-year-old students it increased from 6.7 per cent in 1996 to 15 per cent in 1998. By 2011 these figures are expected to rise to 14 per cent and 25 per cent respectively.
- **Married women**. The percentage of married women working outside the home in paid employment has risen dramatically in recent years (a 6.7 per cent increase for 35–39-year-olds between 1986 and 1998). As Ireland still lags behind other EU states some rise is expected to continue in the near future.

One factor that may slow down the falling ratio is the increasing number of people who seek early retirement. However, this increase many be softened by:
- Increased personal pension contributions as a consequence of recent increased taxation allowances.
- The creation of a new government pension fund to provide old-age pensions.

> **Class activity**
> For your studies so far attempt the following:
> 1. Explain the effects of urbanisation on (a) rural areas; (b) urban areas.
> 2. Explain two major consequences/challenges of the rapid rise in global population.
> 3. Explain two positive effects of Ireland's increasing population.

The cost of supporting increasing numbers in dependency age groups becomes higher as a society moves through the low fluctuating stage

Class activity

Use what you have learned so far to answer the following questions.
1. Give one positive and one negative consequence of improving educational standards of very young children.
2. Suggest two ways in which people aged 65 and older could reduce their degree of dependency on the working population. Give one positive and one negative effect of each of your answers.

SECTION 2 (CHAPTER 5)
CAUSES AND EFFECTS OF OVERPOPULATION

 **Population characteristics have an impact on people's way of life, their families and their living standards.**

Chapter 5 discusses how various population characteristics such as social attitudes, education levels, culture and income affect standards of living. It also investigates how standards of living and the development of resources may impact on population patterns, leading to overpopulation in some regions, while other areas with better planning may thrive and prosper.

- Chapter 5   Overpopulation

Regions of intensive farming can support large numbers of people

Cultural factors often negatively affect the ability of a country to achieve high living standards

The number of elderly people in a country increases as technology and economic conditions improve

25

CHAPTER 5
OVERPOPULATION

WHAT DOES OPTIMUM POPULATION MEAN?

The optimum population of an area is the number of people working with all the available resources of that area who will produce the highest standard of living and quality of life available to them. Theoretically there is an optimum population for every country. This optimum is not the same for every region, as the available resources will change from region to region. So some places have a high optimum population while others may have a lower optimum population. This concept of an optimum population is never static. It will change in every area over time because:

- Technology improves over time (e.g. better methods of exploration, the use of fertilisers).
- Population numbers may change due to emigration.
- Population structure (age and sex structure) may change.
- New discoveries may be made in that area, such as minerals, for example oil or metal ores; or existing deposits may be used up.

WHAT DOES OVERPOPULATION MEAN?

Overpopulation occurs when there are **too many people** in an area for the **resources** of that area to maintain an **adequate standard of living**. So overpopulation does not depend merely upon the total population living in a country, or necessarily upon the density of the population.

For example, **the Netherlands** has an average density of **420 people per square kilometre**. It is not overpopulated.

On the other hand, the **Calabria region in southern Italy** has a population density of only **137 people per square kilometre** and is overpopulated.

The Netherlands has a total population of 15.75 million people in an area the size of Munster in Ireland. It is one of the richest nations of

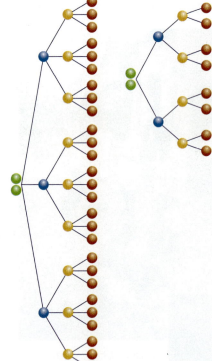

Three-child families   Two-child families

Fig. 5.1

Class activity
In just three generations, three-child families produce more than treble the number of people generated by two-child families.
How may some governments influence family size?
Suggest some disadvantages of this.

the world. In 1990, the Irish Republic had a total population of just 3.5 million people. In that year over 70,000 people emigrated due to unemployment. Therefore **Ireland was overpopulated**, even though it is 1.7 times larger and had only one-quarter of the population of the Netherlands. Between 1995 and 2001 Ireland was under-populated and did not have sufficient workers. The government searched abroad for nurses, teachers and civil servants. Now, with a population of 4.0 million, Ireland's unemployment rate will hopefully remain low.

Thomas Malthus was the first person to draw attention to rising world population. Today, as the world's population grows rapidly, there is a **revival of Malthus's ideas**. Some believe that population numbers will eventually be restricted by limited resources and that genetic engineering and other production techniques are only temporary stopgaps and will not keep pace with population growth.

Who was Thomas Malthus? Search the Web for information about him.

CAUSES AND EFFECTS OF OVERPOPULATION

The Impact of Resource Development
Even in relatively well-off societies, the unwise development of a natural resource can create overpopulation in a region.

Reduced fresh water supply
Case Study: the Aral Sea environment
The Aral Sea is located in central Asia. In 1950, its natural resource of fresh water supply supported mixed agriculture around its shores and a flourishing fishing industry.

The Aral Sea project and its original purpose. The waters of the two largest rivers, the Amu and Syr, which flow through a desert and feed the Aral Sea, were diverted through canals to irrigate seven million hectares of cotton, rice and melon fields for the markets of the former Soviet Union. Though the water diversion was carried out to increase agricultural production, it has only partially done so, but at extreme cost to the local region and its people.

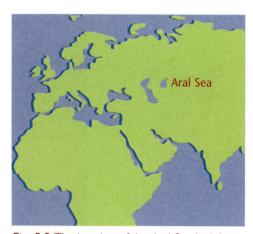

Fig. 5.2 The location of the Aral Sea in Asia

The consequences are:
- The Aral Sea **eco-system**, which was in perfect balance with local natural resources, such as fresh water supplies, fish life, delta farmland and climate, and which sustained a large population, was **destroyed**. This region is now **overpopulated**.
- The fishing industry has been devastated and fishing ports are up to 50 kilometres from the seashore today. Because the waters of the Amu and Syr have been diverted, only a tiny amount of fresh water is reaching the Aral Sea. As the sea

CAUSES AND EFFECTS OF OVERPOPULATION

Fig. 5.3 This sketch shows a shrinking Aral Sea. The original coastline can be up to 80 kilometres from the reduced shoreline.

shrank, the salt content increased dramatically. Twenty fish species have been wiped out. Former fishing communities have been economically devastated, fishermen are no longer needed and beached trawlers lie in dry ports. **Most of the urban populations of these fishing towns have migrated from the region.**

Class activity
Read the account of the Aral Sea project.
1. What was the original aim of the Aral Sea project?
2. How did the project affect
   (a) the livelihoods of the local population;
   (b) the distribution of the local population;
   (c) the wildlife of the region?

Many fishermen kept the local fishing industry alive until there was no longer enough water to keep the fishing boats afloat

Use your atlas to identify the countries that border the Aral Sea.

Too little flood-free farmland
Case Study: subsistence farming in Bangladesh

Bangladesh is one of the poorest and least developed countries on earth, with a population of 128 million people that is growing at a rate of 1.9 per cent each year. Bangladesh is an independent country formed from the double delta of the Ganges and Brahmaputra rivers.

Causes of overpopulation. The land of Bangladesh lies barely above sea level. Its land is a web of distributaries (stream channels) that flow to the sea. The deltas' alluvial

OVERPOPULATION

soils are extremely fertile and every inch of the land is under crops: rice and wheat for food; jute and tea for cash. The rivers' annual floods (due to monsoons) bring silt that piles up to form new islands. Even as this new land builds up, people move in to farm it. Because Bangladesh has a rapidly growing population, the pressure of ever more mouths to feed drives this migration. Bangladesh has a **GDP of US$260 per person**. Only 16 per cent of its population live in cities. It is a land of **subsistence farmers**, who have only **tiny portions of land** to feed their families. Its **infrastructure is poor**. There is not a single road bridge across the Ganges river anywhere in the country and there is only one railway bridge across the river. Many lose their lives each year as overcrowded 'ferries' transport people across the rivers. Bangladesh has too few resources to support its people. Its population growth and lack of advanced farming methods create overpopulation.

Bangladesh, with a population of 128 million, suffers from overcrowding and over-population

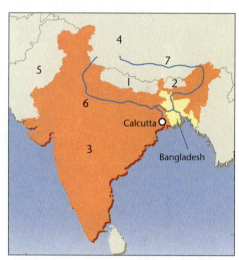

Fig. 5.4 Examine the map. Then identify: (a) the countries 1–5; (b) the rivers 6 and 7 on whose deltas Bangladesh is situated.

Bangladesh suffers from regular flooding, partly as a consequence of deforestation in the headstreams of its major rivers

The rivers of Bangladesh migrate across this fast flood plain – delta region. The main stream alone continuously erodes its banks at a rate of up to 2 km a year, destroying everything in its wake – farmland, factories, hospitals, schools and homes. Managing such a powerful river is almost impossible.

Future Food and Water Supplies

How to provide food and water for a growing population remains another vital concern. Global per capita grain output has been stagnant for more than a decade and crop land is shrinking. **So access to water will be critical.** According to a recent study, one fourth of the world's people are likely to live in countries facing chronic or recurring shortages of fresh water by the year 2050. This may cause some regions to become newly overpopulated.

THE INFLUENCE OF SOCIETY AND CULTURE

Some factors that influence overpopulation and people's quality of life include religious and cultural factors.

Religious Influence

Many of the major religions support family development and oppose artificial birth control and abortion. Consequently, strongly religious societies tend to experience high birth rates, e.g. India and Brazil. For example, Muslim countries and predominantly Catholic countries have high birth rates. Irish birth rates were very high up to the 1960s. This led to overpopulation and subsequent emigration.

Case Study: India – religious and cultural factors
Status of women

An important socio-cultural influence on Calcutta's population is the **high fertility rate of Indian women**. Generally women **marry early**, have **little choice** in the male-arranged marriage, and enter a household with the prime task of producing male heirs for their husband's family name and genes to continue. Mindful of family honour, females are secluded from other males by not working outside the household and often by practising purdah. With **little access to education and employment**, they have little access to family planning advisors.

Fertility ritual in India. Women in India at prayer with a Brahman priest to get a good husband and to give birth to many sons.

> What is 'purdah'? Look up this word in your dictionary.

Cattle – an underused resource

India has the largest concentration of livestock in the world: one-third of the world's cattle on three per cent of the world's land. The economic and social value of cattle as a source of milk and dung were so great in the past that cattle have long been seen as sacred. The Hindu belief that to kill a cow is to make oneself impure leads to cows roaming the cities' streets or being kept in compounds to die. Because of overstocking, overgrazing and a regional lack of fodder, more than 120 million cattle suffer from malnutrition and so are of little value economically. India's sustainable small farming communities are disappearing.

Cultural Influence

The Sertao in north-east Brazil was one of the earliest places in South America to be colonised by the Portuguese. Portuguese planters soon imported the country's largest group of African slaves to work in the sugar fields. This combined foreign population of planters, other Portuguese colonists and African slaves laid the foundation of the difficulties in this region today. This drier inland backcountry – called the **Sertao** – is not only seriously overpopulated but also contains some of the worst poverty to be found anywhere in Central and South America. Much of this region's misery is **rooted in the unequal division of land**, a legacy of the plantation system.

Fig. 5.5 The Sertao region of north-east Brazil

INCOME LEVELS, EDUCATION, TECHNOLOGY AND POPULATION GROWTH

Level of Economic Development

Generally speaking, high birth rates and large families are characteristic of underdeveloped countries. This is attributed to the need to ensure adequate support for parents in their old age, to the general low level of education and limited expectations.

In contrast, where people are well off and levels of education are more advanced, birth control is more feasible and families are often small so as not to interfere with material gain.

Effects of Rising Incomes

The population Transition Model suggests that as people and less developed countries of the South raise their income their birth rates will automatically decline as they have done in rich countries of the North.

The Sertao region has been an area of out-migration for many years

CAUSES AND EFFECTS OF OVERPOPULATION

Age group	No education	Primary	Secondary	Higher
20–24	1.6	1.1	0.7	0.5
25–29	2.7	1.7	1.3	0.9
30–34	3.9	2.6	1.9	1.3
35–39	5.1	3.4	2.4	2.2
40–44	6.1	4.2	3.2	2.7
45–49	6.7	4.9	3.4	2.5

Table 5.1 Average number of children born to Moroccan women according to age and educational level.

Throughout western Europe, as income levels in society increase, family size is reduced

Class activity
1. How many children are born to Moroccan women in the age group:
   (a) 20–24 with (i) no education;
       (ii) higher education?
   (b) 40–49 with (i) no education;
       (ii) higher education?
2. What effect does level of education have on Moroccan women with regard to family size, according to the statistics?

Some Indian families are very rich and can afford high-income lifestyles

This theory was based on the belief that the rapid growth in population numbers in Third World countries was entirely based on rapidly falling death rates due to new medicines etc. But studies **in some countries** have shown that as **income improved so also did fertility rates** and this was a reason for increasing numbers leading to overpopulation in some areas.

Other studies suggest that fertility increases are a common and a universal feature of modernisation. But there are others who maintain that high fertility is so accepted as the norm and is so interwoven with the entire cultural fabric of less developed countries that its reduction is simply impossible.

The increase in fertility in Ireland since 1994 has been attributed to women between the ages of 30 and 39. It is suggested that it is a 'once-off' postponement effect following a steep decline in fertility rates of previous years and is unlikely to continue.

Low Income Leading to Out-Migration

Case Study: the Mezzogiorno in southern Italy – an industrially underdeveloped region

For most of the twentieth century, the southern part of Italy, called the Mezzogiorno, has been overpopulated. Incomes in the Mezzogiorno have traditionally been much lower than in other parts of the country. This southern region suffers from a number of physical and economic disadvantages that cause outmigration.

Because of its intense Mediterranean summer heat and the region's lack of water, its steep Apennine mountain slopes and limited mineral resources, the region has consistently been unable to provide a sufficient income for its population.

The region, which has traditionally had high birth rates, continues to suffer from out-migration and most migrants move to the industrialised core region of northern Italy. Over 5 million people have left the region since 1951, including 1.1 million between 1983 and 1993.

What evidence in this photograph suggests that people in this area have low incomes?

High Income Leading to Optimum Population

Case Study: Japan – an advanced industrial society

Japan has one of the highest physiologic population densities (see page 3) in the world, 3,070 people per square kilometre (7,950 per square mile). It has a population of 127 million. Yet it is not overpopulated and, in addition, the Japanese have the longest life expectancy in the world.

Its 127 million people are crowded into a total area just five times the size of the Irish Republic, most of it mountainous, subject to frequent earthquakes and volcanic eruptions. It has no oil fields, little coal, few raw materials for industry and not much level land for farming. Only 18 per cent of Japan's land is classed as habitable and 79 per cent of its population live in cities.

Intensive cultivation and high output from farmland has always been a priority in Japan

Advanced communications systems indicate the high standards of Japanese people.

How does Japan support such a high population?
Japan has defeated the odds by relying on old Japanese virtues: organisational efficiency, massive productivity, dedication to quality and adherence to common aims.

- Japan has made huge investments in research on high-yielding rice varieties, mechanisation, irrigation, terracing and fertilisation.
- Japan has developed a **fishing** industry that accounts for one-seventh of the world's catch. Japan's coasts have about 4,000 fishing villages and tens of thousands of small fishing boats and trawlers. They also practise aquaculture: the practice of 'farming' freshwater fish in artificial ponds and flooded paddy fields, and oysters, prawns and shrimp in shallow bays.
- Japan is one of the most **industrialised** and industrially efficient countries in the world. Its major industrial city regions include the Tokyo-Yokohama-Kawasaki urban industrial area.

THE IMPACT OF POPULATION GROWTH RATES ON DEVELOPMENT

This man is pictured with five of his six wives and 20 of his 36 children in Cameroon

How exactly does population growth matter to the development of a country?
There is no single answer. Economists who study such matters, unlike laboratory scientists, cannot conduct controlled experiments. Their work relies on surveys that try to determine patterns over time from the examination of many countries and from theories of other disciplines. The following statements briefly outline what most economists researching population change presently accept. In their studies they have included high fertility, population growth and increased human density that relate to economic well-being in the developing world.

There are two main arguments:
1. Slowing population growth tends to make a population better off financially in developing countries over time.
2. Research fails to capture all the economic benefits of lower rates of population growth because it does not account for the high cost that governments would pay if high population growth continued.

In other words, when population growth falls, the state does not have to increase the number of hospitals, schools etc. that it would have to build if high population growth continued. So reduced population growth reduces expense for governments. So taxes remain stable or may be reduced.

Effect of Population Growth on Development

The poorest nations of the world generally have fast-growing populations.

High dependency ratios result when rapid population growth produces large numbers of children and youth relative to the labour force. Governments and families spend far more on children than the children can quickly repay as they are not earning income. Also as modern schooling and health care replaces child labour, household savings decrease, government costs increase and this leads to a cut in a country's GDP (income), so increased education costs a lot in the short term.

> GDP (gross domestic product) is a standard measure of a nation's total output of goods and services by workers and business. Basically the higher the GDP per person the wealthier the country and its citizens.

Adult education helps women to have greater control over their own lives

> A large number of young people may lead to high unemployment when they reach the age of employment.

High fertility and poverty

Many people are convinced that there are **links** between **high fertility** and resulting population growth on the one hand and **persistent poverty** and low wages in developing countries on the other. Large families associated with high population growth appear to transmit poverty across generations. Because poor people in developing countries have large families their incomes are consistently low. In addition, the availability of a large cheap workforce in some countries slows the introduction of newer, more efficient technology.

There is substantial evidence that having smaller families increases families' savings. A significant part of economic growth achieved among the newly industrialised countries of Asia results from the wise savings created by families.

At family level the ability to plan the number and timing of child births can dramatically effect the quality of life through improved mother and child health, and more productive use of time, energy and income. Women stand to increase earnings the most, although their low status in some societies often limits this opportunity.

What advantages and disadvantages are created by high population densities in places such as Bangladesh and India?

The rate of population growth and the size of a country's income matter. Even in the case of countries that can adjust, it is recognised that it takes time and effort for government and other institutions to:

- Expand urban transport and communications.
- Provide new and better health and educational services.
- Successfully introduce new technology.
- Enforce environmental regulations and expand trade.

Developing countries in which the population growth eases through declines in birth rate will be more likely to increase income and will have more time to create needed jobs.

Class activity

1. Identify two ways that religion and culture influence low income levels in India.
2. Explain two ways that cultural influences in the Sertao in north-east Brazil has led to low incomes in that area. In your answer refer to
   (a) reasons for size of population;
   (b) ownership of land.
3. Explain two reasons for high birth rates (large families) in developing countries.
4. Identify and explain two effects of low incomes in the Mezzogiorno.
5. (a) Explain three ways that Japan has developed to support its large population.
   (b) Explain why Japan has such a small amount of level agricultural land.
       (Hint: island arc, see your *Our Dynamic World 1*.)

Class activity

1. Explain one positive and one negative impact of population growth on
   (a) social development and (b) economic development.
2. Explain the economic advantages to a country's development of slow population growth.
3. Explain how high fertility rates are believed to affect persistent poverty.

SECTION 3 (CHAPTERS 6–8)
MIGRATION

KEY IDEA! Population movements have an impact on the donor and receiver regions.

This section examines how Ireland has since 1950 experienced alternate times of emigration and immigration that related to corresponding periods of recession and growth. It examines migration policies in Ireland and the EU and how these policies affect population movements. Using case studies, it explains various ethnic, racial and religious issues that arise from migration, and examines the contrasting impact of rural-urban migration movements in developed and developing countries.

- Chapter 6   Changing Migration Patterns
- Chapter 7   Ethnic, Racial and Religious Issues Created by Migration
- Chapter 8   Rural to Urban Migration in the Developed and Developing World

High-tech jobs in urban regions have increased rural to urban migration

Shanty towns cover vast areas on the outskirts of cities in the developing world

Racial conflict occurs for many reasons. However, skin colour and religious issues are the most common reasons for prejudice between groups.

37

CHAPTER 6
CHANGING MIGRATION PATTERNS

Refugees in Kosovo as a consequence of war. Does this photograph show voluntary or forced migration?

People have always been prone to wander and to adapt to all kinds of environments. Because environments on the earth's surface are extremely varied and also change from time to time they have resulted in people moving from place to place. This has happened throughout the whole of human history and is still happening today.

The term **migration** is normally used to describe **the movement of people to live in another place for more than a year**. This topic focuses on long-term or permanent changes in peoples' place of residence. Emigration (leaving a country) and immigration (settling in a new country) is usually what we think of in this regard. But permanent movement within national boundaries is probably more significant than either of these in today's world.

VOLUNTARY OR FORCED MIGRATION

It may be difficult to say whether a particular person's migration was forced or voluntary. In some cases, people are forced to flee for their lives. Others, however, choose to leave because they feel they would be able to live better lives elsewhere, maybe among people with similar cultures or beliefs. Nevertheless, we refer to all migrations that are not forced as voluntary migrations. This means that the migrants make a positive choice to move and weigh up the advantages and disadvantages of leaving what they know behind. This must be balanced against the difficulties of their new life ahead and the rewards that they hope it will bring.

Push and Pull Factors

The migrant's destination is said to have a 'pull' effect and one's homeland is seen as having a 'push' effect when one is thinking of moving. There may be conflicting forces: some may suggest that the person would be better to stay, others that the person would profit by leaving.

Each time someone emigrates they have decided that the pull factor is in their favour. This may depend on their age, education and expectations of life and all these will set different weights on the pros and cons of the move. This may depend on how flexible and adventurous they are. Young people, for example, generally adapt to change more easily and rapidly than older people.

Access to information regularly plays an important part in voluntary migration. People who feel sure of their information are likely to weigh up the advantages of moving much more positively than others who are frightened of the unknown. In the case of Irish people in the twentieth century, letters, phone calls and regular comfortable transport all helped to promote migration even when push factors had declined.

Carefully study this photograph and that on page 38. Then discuss the differences in these people's reasons for migration.

MIGRATION IN IRELAND

The population distribution in Ireland has been dominated by two main factors since famine times. These factors are:
- Migration from Ulster, Connacht and Munster to Leinster and abroad.
- Rural to urban migration.

The population distribution of Ireland today is very different from what it was in the nineteenth century. In 1841 the province of **Connacht** had over **1.4 million people**. Today it has just **433,000**. This represents a 70 per cent fall in population. Leinster, on the other hand, had a population of 1,973,731 in 1841. Today it has roughly the same number. With the exception of Leinster, the other three provinces have experienced massive depopulation since that time.

Migration from Ulster, Connacht and Munster to Leinster since 1926

Leinster has continued to increase its percentage share of the total population at each consecutive census since 1926. The remaining three provinces have each continued to lose population over the same period. Leinster's share of total population increased from 38.7 per cent in 1926 to 53.8 per cent in 2002. The shares of Ulster (part of which is in the Irish Republic) and Connacht declined by about one-third over the same seventy-year period, while the fall in Munster's share from 32.6 per cent to 28.2 per cent was less pronounced.

> Remember the two factors responsible for Ireland's present population density and distribution pattern.
> - Migration from Ulster, Connacht and Munster to Leinster and overseas.
> - Rural to urban migration.

MIGRATION

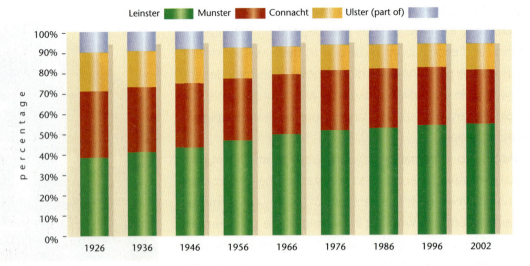

Fig. 6.1 Provincial population shares, 1926–2002

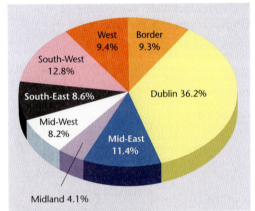

Fig. 6.2 Projected population shares of Regional Authorities, 2031

Class activity
Carefully study Figure 6.1.
1. How do the percentages for each province in 1926 compare to the present-day populations for these areas? (Have they increased or decreased and by how much?)
2. Give some reasons for this decrease (a) in Connacht and (b) in Munster.
3. When was the lowest population percentage reached for (a) Leinster (b) Ulster (c) Munster and (d) Connacht?
4. What patterns are evident from these figures for each region?
5. What overall pattern of change is evident from the percentage share of Ireland's population for each province?
6. What similarities, if any, exist between the patterns in your answer in questions 4 and 5?

Class activity
Carefully study the chart in Figure 6.2.
1. What overall effect will migration and natural increase in 2031 have on Ireland's population in (a) the Dublin region (b) the Eastern region (c) the West?
2. How will this trend affect western regions over time?

Rural to Urban Migration and Subsequent Growth of Irish Cities

The distribution of the population between urban and rural areas has undergone a major change over the last 70 years. Figure 6.3 shows the percentage change of urban/rural population in 1926, 1961 and 2003.

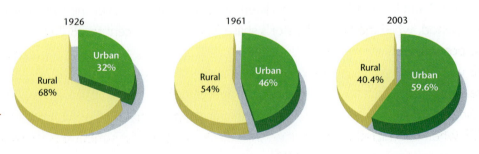

Fig. 6.3 Less than one-third of the population lived in urban areas in 1926. The urban share has increased at each census since then, though the rate of increase has been tapering off in recent times. The 1971 census was the first in which the urban population exceeded the rural. By 2003 approximately 60 per cent of the Irish population were living in urban areas.

40

The growth of urban areas in Ireland, especially over the past 40 years, has been mainly due to:

Industrial estates

The development of industrial estates in urban areas and the increase in industrial jobs over that period has attracted many people, and especially young adults, to cities and towns. Other factors include the increase in commercial, financial and social services in towns and cities.

Accommodation

The construction of attractive suburban houses in well-designed estates that are near to essential services such as schools, universities, leisure centres and hospitals has contributed to urban growth. In addition, high-quality apartments and town houses in renewed urban centres also attract young people to cities.

Third-level education

A large percentage of Ireland's young adults continue their education at third level, including universities and regional colleges. Due to demand for accommodation, large housing estates have developed near these centres of education, especially in our largest cities where most colleges are located.

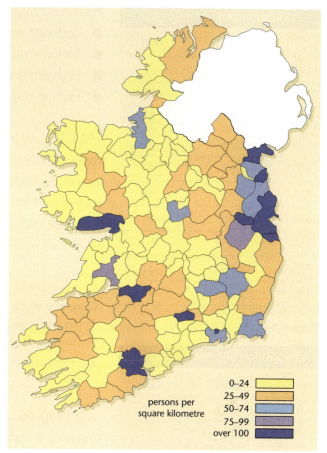

Fig. 6.4 Population density of rural districts, 2003

Class activity

Study the population density of rural districts, including some that surround major Irish towns and cities.
1. In what regions of Ireland are the rural areas that have the lowest population densities?
2. Why have these areas such low population densities? Explain fully.
3. What location factor is common to all rural areas that have the highest density of population?
4. Why have the areas in question 3 such high population densities? Explain fully.
5. What location factor is common to most areas that have a population density of 100 or more persons per square kilometre? Explain fully.

Post-1950 Migration Trends to and from Ireland

The population of the Irish Republic in 1951 was approximately 2.9 million people. This was a fall of over 3.5 million people since 1841, some four years before the Great Famine. Emigration was the main contributory factor in this decline; and this decline continued into the twentieth century. The highest emigration rate occurred in 1958 when net migration figures reached 58,000 people. Throughout the 1950s there was a total net migration of 409,000 people. Emigration in this decade was responsible for the historically low population level of 2.8 million people recorded in 1961.

Why did so many people emigrate during the 1950s and previous decades?

Post-1960 migration patterns created the following trends:
- Reduced emigration during the 1960s to as little as 5,000 in 1971.
- Net in-migration from 1972 to 1979.
- High emigration from 1980 to 1991.
- High in-migration from 1995 to 2000.

1962–79. Ireland experienced its own industrial revolution in the 1960s. Foreign multi-national companies were attracted to Ireland by financial incentives, such as tax-free industrial exports, grants and modern industrial estates for footloose industries. Industrial emigration slowed and by the 1970s there was net in-migration for the first time in the twentieth century. This trend continued until 1979.

Population and net migration		
	,000	,000
1951	2,961	−35
1952	2,953	−35
1953	2,949	−33
1954	2,941	−36
1955	2,921	−45
1956	2,898	−48
1957	2,885	−41
1958	2,853	−58
1959	2,846	−32
1960	2,832	−41

Table 6.1 Migration figures 1951–60

Class activity
Carefully study Tables 6.1 and 6.2.
1. In which year was Ireland's emigration rate highest?
2. In which year were there more *immigrants* than *emigrants* for the first time?
3. How did the migration trend before 1958 differ from that after 1958?

1980–95. An international recession caused a reversal of Ireland's migration trend of the 1960s and 1970s. Many factories were closed or scaled down. There was a net out-migration of 20,000 people in 1985 alone. A revival in international financial markets created a change in Ireland's migration pattern once more, and out-migration started to decline.

1996–2000. Ireland's industrial rise from the low of the 1980s was unprecedented. Its economy boomed and the demand for labour was such that foreign nationals were sought by semi-state companies and the Civil Service to fill job vacancies. Over 20,000 immigrants came to Ireland in 2000.

2000–2002. Net immigration (the balance between in- and out-migration) reached a historical high point of 41,000 in the year to April 2002.

The number of immigrants increased to 66,900 in the year to April 2002 while the number of emigrants declined to a record low of 20,700 in 2003.

Population and net migration		
	,000	,000
1971	2,978	−5
1972	3,024	11
1973	3,073	13
1974	3,124	16
1975	3,177	20
1976	3,228	16
1977	3,272	10
1978	3,314	7
1979	3,368	16

Table 6.2 Migration figures 1971–79

Population and net migration		
	,000	,000
1995	3,601	−2
1996	3,626	8
1997	3,661	19
1998	3,705	17
2000	3,787	26
2001	3,838	33
2002	3,917	41
2003	3,979	29.8

Table 6.3 Migration figures 1995–2003

Class activity
Carefully study the migration statistics in Table 6.3.
1. In which year did out-migration end during the 1990s?
2. Why did this change in population movement occur?
3. Suggest reasons why there was a significant increase of migrants into Ireland towards the end of the 1990s.

Class activity
Examine Figure 6.5. Then do the following:
1. What do net migration figures mean?
2. Identify the most recent trend in Ireland's net migration figures.
3. In which five-year period was Ireland's net migration figures at their lowest level?
4. Account for the trend in net migration during the 1950s and 1980s.

Census year	State population
1901	3,221,823
1911	3,139,688
1926	2,971,992
1936	2,968,420
1946	2,955,107
1951	2,960,593
1956	2,898,264
1961	2,818,341
1966	2,884,002
1971	2,978,248
1979	3,368,217
1981	3,443,405
1986	3,540,643
1991	3,525,719
2000	3,626,087
2003	4,000,000

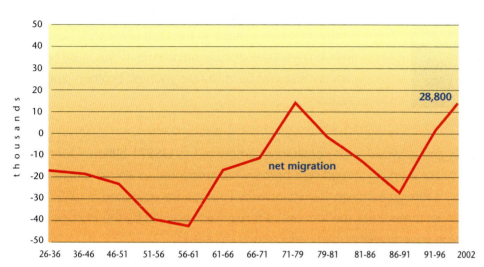

Fig. 6.5 Components of population changes, 1926–2002

Table 6.4 Ireland's population 1901–2003

Class activity
1. In which decade did Ireland's population rise since famine times?
2. Give reasons for the recent rapid rise in Ireland's population.

Effects of Migration in Ireland and Abroad
Some positive effects of emigration

- **Safety valve.** Emigration provided Ireland with the solution to its oldest problem, a lack of jobs for its people. Past governments failed miserably to increase employment sufficiently to provide a decent living for Irish people at home. This was true until the mid-1990s when the 'tiger economy' temporarily reversed this situation. Emigration provided successive Irish governments with a 'safety valve' that reduced total population numbers throughout the twentieth century, and especially during the 1950s and 1980s. Had emigration not occurred then, a population with **high birth rates** and an **increasing unemployment** problem would have **increased pressure** on Ireland's resources at a time when it would not have been able to deal with such a situation. Indeed Ireland has experienced a unique situation in its population structure. While other national populations in the EU grew, Ireland's population was in decline even though it had one of the highest birth rates in Western Europe.

> Ireland was by no means unique in terms of emigration acting as a safety valve. There was a total of 750,000 emigrants from Norway and 1,100,000 from Sweden between 1840 and 1914, equivalent to 40 per cent and 25 per cent respectively of each country's natural increase during that period.

In the past, many ships that sailed from Ireland were packed with immigrants

- **Political rivals**. Countries (populations) or governments or both can also benefit when politically unwanted people emigrate.
- **Remittances and tourism**. Throughout the twentieth century, and continuing today, many emigrant countries earned substantial income from 'remittances', money sent by emigrants or guest workers, called '**Gastarbeiter**' in Germany, to their homeland. This was very much a reality in the case of Ireland. Many Irish emigrants, especially before the 1960s, sent home money that was used to rear younger brothers and sisters.

In **1990**, annual world-wide remittances amounted to **US$71 billion**. During the 1990s, Egyptians working abroad sent home what amounted to almost a third of their country's foreign earnings. Remittances by Filipinos are estimated at US$8 billion annually, almost three times the amount of foreign aid received by the Philippines. The Philippine government publicly encourages this trend.

Is it not strange to think that just a short time ago we were in this situation?

Many Irish emigrants were successful in the construction industry in Britain and America

Recent improvements in employment opportunities offer a bright future for Ireland's young people

Some negative effects of emigration

- **Loss of skilled workforce**. A careful examination of the age-sex pyramid for 1961, Figure 4.7, page 19, shows that a large number of people between the ages of 16 and 40 were absent from the Irish workforce. These ages make up the most youthful and energetic groups in a population's workforce. The absence of such people limits a nation's ability to increase productivity and change; so income levels remain low.

    This is referred to as '**The Brain Drain**'. In the 1950s and 1960s this was commonly seen as a problem for developing countries, such as Turkey, Greece, Spain, Portugal and Ireland, that lost their citizens through migration.

- **Smaller home market**. A large number of young adults in a country increases the demand (a market) for numerous products. They have disposable income and are among the largest spenders, which creates a demand for manufactured goods. If people emigrate it reduces this home market.
- **Depopulation**. The West of Ireland suffers from a number of **environmental disadvantages**. Much of the West comprises **highland** and **extensive mountain areas**. Much of this is covered by **blanket bog** and much of the soil is too wet. Farms are small and uneconomic. In the past mass emigration

from these regions left the area without its young and able workers. Farms were left in charge of an **ageing,** low-output population. Market towns and villages, such as Ballina and Foxford in County Mayo, struggled for survival. As people left, services became fewer as there were insufficient numbers of local people with enough disposable income to support them. This in turn created a cycle of decline from which the West is still struggling to recover.

Some positive effects of immigration

Foreign migrants. At present Ireland is suffering a shortage of labour in certain areas, such as nursing and some civil service departments. Foreign skilled workers are sought after by Irish government agencies and they have been somewhat successful in attracting some professionals such as nurses from the Philippines. Many other migrant workers are in paid employment as waitresses and shop assistants. This situation has helped Ireland to fill lower paid employment not sought after by locals.

- **Cultural effects.** Migrants may enhance a culture by making it more outward looking and cosmopolitan, especially in the case of a peripheral island nation such as Ireland. Because Ireland has for so long been a place of emigration rather than immigration people from only a few different cultures have settled here up to now. Most of these are associated with the food industry, such as Chinese, Indian and Thai people, and the medical profession, such as doctors and nurses from such countries as India, the Philippines and some African nations. Nowadays, however, people from other regions are entering Ireland in ever-growing numbers. Many of these people are refugees from politically oppressed areas such as Kosovo (part of former Yugoslavia) and Nigeria.
- **New skills.** Foreign nationals also bring new skills to a country. These skills vary depending on the levels of economic development of the nations from which they come. Many of Ireland's university graduates and skilled tradespeople learned new skills and industrial work practices while working overseas.

Many foreign nationals fill job vacancies in Ireland. What positive effects can such migrants have on Irish society?

Some negative effects of immigration

- **Repatriation of guest workers.** When foreign nationals are employed it is generally on a fixed-contract basis and their numbers are closely watched in relation to trends of demand and need. In Germany, such workers were called Gasterbeiter (guest workers), which suggests that they were there for a short period only and that when they were no longer needed they could be sent home, even if they had a family who had adjusted to that society. The fall of Communism and the unification of East and West Germany caused many financial and social difficulties, including unemployment within Germany. Right-wing groups in some cases blamed the guest workers for their unemployment difficulties. This led to racist attacks on the homes of guest workers.

- **Refugees.** Wars, ethnic hatred and different living standards have created a large percentage of African international migration since the Second World War. Independence from colonial rule in Africa led to civil wars within nations and to conflicts between nations. In the last two decades millions of refugees have fled to neighbouring countries to escape civil wars. In 1999, Guinea, with a population of only 7.5 million people, cared for 700,0000 refugees from civil wars in four neighbouring countries.

By 1999 Africa, with only 12 per cent of the world's population, had more than 20 per cent of the world's refugees. In all such cases, the cost of supporting such enormous numbers of refugees can cause a serious strain on the host country, not just financially but also socially, as many refugees in some refugee camps may be from opposing sides.

Ethnic and racial conflicts also occur as a consequence of migration. See Chapter 7.

Use your PC to find out about current refugees.

Children are often the ones who suffer most as a consequence of ethnic conflict. Their educational and social needs may not be met at a time when they are most vulnerable.

What is a refugee? A refugee is someone who has left his or her own country or is unable to return to it owing to a well-founded fear of persecution for reasons of race, religion, nationality, membership of a particular group or political opinion.

Class activity
1. Explain three positive effects of immigration for Ireland in the past.
2. Explain three negative effects of emigration for Ireland in the past.
3. Explain two positive effects of immigration for Ireland at present.
4. Explain two negative effects of repatriation for foreign nationals who may have to return home from Ireland.

MIGRATION POLICIES IN THE EUROPEAN UNION AND IRELAND

Migration Policies in the European Union

Ever since 1957, the treaty establishing the European Union has contained articles to ensure the free movement of workers within the community. This idea of the free movement of persons has gradually become established by means of treaties between EU members. Since 1993, all European citizens have the right to move and live anywhere within the EU. The reason for this policy is because '**the mobility of labour within the community must be one of the means by which the worker is guaranteed the possibility of improving his living and working conditions, and promoting his social advancement**'.

Also, the freedom to take up a job in another member state of the EU must not be put at risk and migrant workers are entitled to remain in the territory of a member state after working there.

Some member states have interpreted the meaning of this principle differently. For some, it applied only to community citizens, so border controls were still needed to check the identity of nationals of non-member countries. For others, it applied to everyone, so internal border controls were no longer necessary. After long discussion, only Ireland and the United Kingdom have not signed up to this agreement. In future, this principle will have to be adopted by all new member states.

Migration policies allow EU citizens to travel freely within the Union, while others may or may not be allowed enter or remain

The European Union's asylum policy

The country that must take responsibility for awarding refugee status to an individual will be the country in which the asylum seeker first arrives. It has been agreed to establish a database (Eurodac) designed to collect fingerprints of asylum seekers and illegal immigrants, to decide the country responsible and to speed up and process claims.

Part of the difficulty of accepting some refugees is that some people from countries that were colonies of European powers have citizenship rights in these European countries. Other countries, such as Ireland, that were not colonial powers are reluctant to take responsibility for citizens of these colonies who seek refuge as a consequence of ethnic conflict at home. A special fund was established in 1998, allowing the EU to grant financial aid to improve facilities and services for the processing of refugee claims and to help in their voluntary return if conditions improve at home.

The enormous increase in recent years of refugee numbers has put added pressure on countries such as Ireland to accept their appropriate share of this problem. In addition, the increase in illegal immigration and trafficking in human beings has become an extra burden in processing claims for political asylum.

> The greatest difficulty with regard to refugees is economic migrants, who are not so much fleeing persecution as seeking to improve their standard of living and using refugee status to get around immigration barriers.

Ireland's immigration policy

The main components of Ireland's immigration policy include:

- Nationals from the European Economic Area (EEA) do not need a visa to live and work in Ireland. The EEA consists of the EU states plus Norway, Iceland and Leichtenstein. For all others, a visa is essential.
- Those who need a visa must apply for a work permit before they enter the state.
- Persons who claim asylum are given full board accommodation while their claim is being processed, initially in Dublin and later at recognised centres throughout Ireland.
- Those who do not require a visa include:
  1. Persons who have permission to remain in Ireland, such as people with special skills and foreign full-time students.
  2. Persons who have refugee status.
  3. Persons who have been granted permission to remain on humanitarian grounds.
  4. Persons who are claiming refugee status while their claim is being processed.

Class activity

1. Explain two ways that freedom from movement within the EU has benefited Irish people.
2. How has the increase in trafficking in human beings affected:
   (a) many vulnerable young females?
   (b) other male or female emigrants who may have participated in this process?
   (c) the countries of their final destination?
   (d) the countries where they came from originally?
3. Do you agree or disagree with Ireland's present policy on immigration? Explain your answer fully.
4. What is meant by 'political asylum'? Explain.

CHAPTER 7
ETHNIC, RACIAL AND RELIGIOUS ISSUES CREATED BY MIGRATION

Let us begin this chapter by understanding the meaning of the terms 'race' and 'ethnic'.

RACE

Race is a word that refers to biological inheritance. We are born with it. It refers to our physical characteristics, such as skin colour, height, physique, hair type, head shape and so on. They belong to our DNA characteristics that are passed on from generation to generation, from parents to offspring. But one thing is sure, there is no such thing as a pure race. We can see that some people have similar characteristics. For example, the people of Scandinavia are generally blue-eyed, fair-haired, fair-skinned people. This is probably because, historically, people have moved out of, rather than in to Scandinavia, so there has been less mixing of migrant groups in this region. The Aborigines were cut off on an isolated continent for so long that they are physically distinctive.

What evidence in this photograph indicates that Irish people have mixed genetic ancestry?

However, look around your own classroom. How many students have similar characteristics? Probably none. Some are brown-haired, others red-haired, black-haired, fair-haired, blond-haired: fair-skinned, sallow-skinned; brown-eyed, blue-eyed, grey-eyed and so on. Therefore it is obvious we have inherited varied characteristics through the generations from migrant groups that have settled in Ireland.

However, people regularly suffer discrimination based on skin colour alone or skin colour, eye shape and hair colour.

> Recent new laws in Ireland help to prevent discrimination on the grounds of race, colour, nationality or ethnic origin. The basic principle states that 'people should be judged on their merits as individuals rather than by reference to the group to which they belong'.

ETHNICITY

'Ethnic' or 'ethnicity' generally refers to a minority group with a collective self-identity within a larger host population, for example Italians in New York, Cubans in Miami or Chinese in Ireland. Due to insecurity or by force they may be found in 'ethnic islands' or 'ghettos'. The Irish are associated with the Bronx in New York and Camden Town in London. The Irish lived near to each other, they helped each other. Simple, uncomplicated, natural.

Such minority groups may be defined by:
- **Place of birth.** In many countries people may be classified on official records by their place of birth or that of their ancestors, such as Chinese, Puerto Rican, African American or American-Irish.

MIGRATION

Class activity
Explain the meaning of the terms
(a) race;
(b) ethnic.

- **Language and fertility rates.** Language may also be used to classify ethnic groups, such as Hispanics in the USA (migrants from Spanish-speaking-American countries, such as Mexico and Central America), who have been grouped by their common language and high fertility rates.
- **Religion.** Some ethnic groups, such as Muslims and Sikhs, prefer to be classified by their religion.

RACIAL DIVISION

Case Study: apartheid in South Africa

Apartheid was **racial separation of blacks from whites as a principle of society enforced by law** and by government policy in South Africa. Centuries ago Dutch and British settlers colonised and controlled this region. In 1931, Britain gave South Africa full independence. During this time and before 1948 racial segregation was widely practised. But in 1948 a policy of **racial discrimination became law** and was given the name 'apartheid'. Under this policy a minority of white people controlled a majority of black and coloured people. This racial discrimination by law ended only in the 1990s.

Fig. 7.1 South Africa is highlighted

Apartheid imposed appallingly heavy burdens on most South Africans. The economic gap between the wealthy few, nearly all of whom were white, and the poor masses, virtually all of whom were African, coloured or Indian, was larger than in any other country. At its height in 1970, there were 15 million Africans, 2 million coloureds (people of mixed African, white and Asian descent), 600,000 Asians and only 3.7 million whites in South Africa. The whites were well-fed, well-housed and well-cared-for. The non-white majority suffered from widespread poverty, malnutrition and disease.

Apartheid laws affected every aspect of life in South Africa.

Apartheid ended in 1994 after 50 years of racial inequality

Non-whites could not buy land. The master plan of apartheid was the 'Homelands Policy'. By this policy all Africans were relocated to deprived, almost uninhabited parts of the country. Once there, they lost 'citizenship' of South Africa.

Apartheid ended in 1994 when all South Africans, whites and non-whites elected their new government. However, the social and economic effects of apartheid continue today.

> **Class activity**
> 1. What was apartheid?
> 2. How did it affect the majority of people in South Africa?
> 3. When did apartheid end?

Irish Attitudes to Refugees

Psychologist Patricia Casey suggests attitudes may simply reflect the reaction of a people slow to change.

The findings of the opinion poll in relation to our attitudes to refugees make for interesting and potentially worrying conclusions. However, all is not as gloomy as first impressions suggest, and comparisons with an earlier survey show a shift towards more tolerance.

When questioned as to whether the Government's response to the refugee situation has been too lax or too strict, 53 per cent felt it was too lax and 29 per cent said it was about right. The remainder either had no opinion or felt it was too strict.

Dublin was the least tolerant, with 61 per cent feeling the Government approach was too lax, and Connacht/Ulster the most tolerant, with only 41 per cent expressing this opinion.

Only 17 per cent overall welcomed the development of a multi-cultural society and 34 per cent believed Irish people should get preferential treatment over foreigners, a view that found most support among the unemployed (49 per cent) and the over-65 age group (46 per cent).

Twenty-four per cent of those polled felt foreigners should be treated exactly the same way as Irish people and a further 20 per cent were fearful of a rise in racist incidents.

It is all too tempting to suggest that the findings in the present poll represent xenophobia and that they are based on an innate dislike or even hatred of people

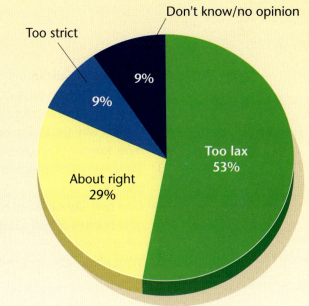

Fig. 7.2 The results of an *Irish Independent* poll, 19 December 2000

from other cultures, and especially of different skin-colour. However, this is all too glib an explanation; nobody has suggested that the Irish claim to be superior morally, intellectually or in any other way to non-nationals, yet this is the basis of xenophobia.

The record of the Irish in helping others assailed by famine or floods, and our enthusiasm to welcome into our families orphans from countries afflicted by dire poverty, belies the perception that we are innately racist.

Indeed, we have always been more than happy to have doctors from other cultures treat us in our hospitals and we have lived amicably with the thriving Chinese community who introduced us to, and modified their cuisine, to suit our palates.

Perhaps the attitudes that are being highlighted in this poll represent a fear of change rather than a hatred of other cultures. We have always been a conservative people, slow to adopt habits and values that are perceived as different.

It is only in the last 10 years or so that ethnic food has become readily available in our supermarkets and restaurants. Until recently, our children remained at home until marriage, and the creche culture is a new phenomenon.

Likewise, the change from being homogenous to multi-cultural represents an enormous shift and, as with any major change, people become fearful and insecure.

Extract taken from the *Irish Independent*, Saturday 30 December 2000.

Class activity

Read the extract above.
1. What evidence in the extract suggests that Irish people are tolerant of other nationalities and willing to help refugees?
2. Suggest why the Dublin region seems to be the least tolerant and Connacht/Ulster the most tolerant of refugees.
3. Explain why Irish people in the past have been slow to adopt change in traditional values and habits.
4. Give two fully explained reasons why refugees can play an important part in the development of Irish society in the twenty-first century.
5. What is xenophobia?
6. What effects can rapid change in migration patterns have on a population?

Class activity

1. Define what you understand by the term 'Irish'.
2. What opposition/racism did Irish emigrants experience in some countries in the past?
3. Which groups of immigrants are more likely to suffer racial abuse in Ireland?
4. Why have Irish attitudes changed in recent years to some foreign immigrants?
5. What do you understand by the term 'economic migrant'?

ETHNIC, RACIAL AND RELIGIOUS ISSUES CREATED BY MIGRATION

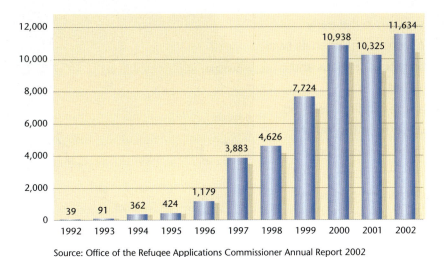

Source: Office of the Refugee Applications Commissioner Annual Report 2002

Fig. 7.3 Ireland's refugee applications 1992–2002

Class activity
Carefully study the chart in Figure 7.3.
1. Identify the trend in refugee applications for this period.
2. Identify one positive effect of this trend on (a) Ireland's population structure and (b) Irish attitudes to other cultures.
3. Give one reason for the trend identified in your answer to question 1.

ETHNIC CLEANSING

This term was first used during the wars following the break-up of former Yugoslavia. It describes a policy where ethnic groups are expelled by force, threat or terror from a territory in which they live so that it can be exclusively occupied by the most powerful group. The deliberate elimination of the Muslim people from Bosnia-Herzegovina through forced out-migration or worse by the Serb army led to ethnic cleansing in many areas. The slaughter of entire populations of many valleys and towns, such as the massacre of Srebrenica, and the creation of enclaves (small pockets/areas occupied by ethnic groups) during these wars by the Serbs were a stark reminder of the Holocaust.

Use a PC to find out more about the Tutsi in Rwanda.

Case Study: the Indian sub-continent – an ethnic and religious conflict

As a consequence of colonisation by the British, Great Britain once ruled the region that is now Pakistan, India and Bangladesh. During the 1800s and early 1900s all three countries formed India. The British ruled India, as they did other lands, by a 'divide and conquer' strategy. They promoted religious, ethnic and cultural divisions among their colonies to keep them under their control.

Mass graves were discovered in Bosnia after genocide by the Serbs

Independence movements in India gained strength in the early 1900s and differences between its two major religious groups, Hindus and Muslims, increased.

Almost all the Muslims believed the Hindus would have too much power over them if India gained independence from Britain. In 1940, the Muslims demanded partition of India along religious lines. The British and Hindus rejected the idea. Consequently, riots occurred between Hindus and Muslims. In 1947 the British and Hindu leaders finally agreed to partition. When the British granted independence to India in 1947, they divided the country according to the religion of its people. **Most Pakistanis are Muslim while most Indians are Hindu.**

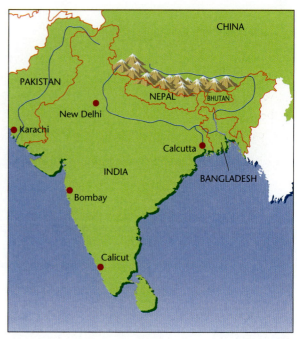

Fig. 7.4 The Indian sub-continent

Pakistan was created in two parts: one to the east of India, called East Pakistan; and the other to the west of India, called West Pakistan. Although the people of both parts of Pakistan shared the same religion – they were mostly Muslim – there were many differences of culture, language and ethnicity.

Fighting between Hindus and Muslims continued in Pakistan and India after partition. Great social unrest caused many people to fear for their safety. So push factors forced many Hindus (6 million) in Pakistan to flee to India while many Muslims (7 million) in India fled to Pakistan. Thousands died during this migration. Then India and Pakistan went to war over a neighbouring state, Kashmir, that had remained independent after partition. This dispute continues today.

The recent mass migration of ethnic groups has led to the creation of multi-cultural societies in many parts of the world. In most countries there is at least one minority group. While such a group may be able to live in peace and harmony with the majority group, unfortunately it is more likely that there will be prejudice and discrimination, leading to conflicts.

> The Indian sub-continent is a natural region, see page 15 in *Our Dynamic World 1*.

Mahatma Gandhi worked for peaceful co-existence between Muslims and Hindus in India

Why not show the film *Gandhi* in class? This will help you to learn how religious conflict can arise between two peoples.

Other conflicts have arisen within the Indian sub-continent. These include those between Tamils and Sinhalese in Sri Lanka, Sikhs and Hindus, and Chinese and Indians.

Racial conflicts also exist, such as those between Aryans and Dravidians: see *Aryan-Dravidian Controversy* by David Frawley. Type these words into a search engine.

The differences between the people of East Pakistan and West Pakistan led to civil war in 1971. As a consequence, East Pakistan became an independent nation called Bangladesh. Over 1 million people died in this war.

Class activity

1. When, in the twentieth century, was India divided into separate states?
2. Who controlled India up until this time?
3. Why was India divided into separate states?
4. Why did migration continue after the newly independent states were established?

CHAPTER 8
RURAL TO URBAN MIGRATION IN THE DEVELOPED AND DEVELOPING WORLD

KEY IDEA! Migration has affected rural areas that people leave behind and cites where they arrive.

CONTRASTING IMPACTS OF RURAL-URBAN MIGRATION IN DEVELOPED AND DEVELOPING AREAS

Rural poverty has forced millions of people in India into the cities in search of a better life

Urban growth processes, and consequently their impacts, in the world's developing countries have been entirely different from those in developed regions. Cities in developed countries are self-supporting areas that developed as a consequence of industrialisation. The growth of industry and industrial estates within urban areas attracted rural dwellers to take up employment in towns and cities. In other words, urban development was created as a consequence of industrialisation: the **industrialisation came first and then the cities grew** because of industrialisation.

However, the urbanisation of developing countries has been a consequence of population growth and rural to urban migration that preceded industrialisation: the **cities came first and then industry developed slowly** within these cities. This has happened because urban growth has been driven by 'rural push' forces rather than 'urban pull' forces of prospective jobs in towns and cities that occur in urban areas of the developed world.

In much of the developing world, rural populations that grew quickly as a consequence of reducing death rates with continuing high birth rates, face a difficult if not hopeless future of drudgery and poverty. In the past, emigration provided a safety valve, but most developed countries have prevented immigration by restricting migrants by various means and for as many reasons. The only hope for the growing numbers of

Do you remember the Demographic Transition Model from your Junior Certificate course?

impoverished rural dwellers has been to move to relatively nearby towns and cities. Here at least there is hope of employment, the prospect of access to schools, health clinics, a safe water supply and other kinds of public facilities and services that are often unavailable in rural areas.

Overall, the cities of the developing world have absorbed four out of five of the 1.2 billion city dwellers who have been added to the world's population since 1970.

IMPACTS OF RURAL TO URBAN MIGRATION IN DEVELOPING COUNTRIES

Rapid Urban Population Growth

Rural migrants have poured into cities out of desperation and hope, rather than having been drawn by jobs and opportunities. Because these migrations have mostly been composed of teenagers and young adults, an important additional impact has been exceptionally **high rates of natural population increase** (high birth rates with low death rates). In most developing countries the rate of natural increase of urban populations exceeds the rate of net in-migration. On average, about 60 per cent of current urban population growth in developing countries is caused by natural increase within the cities.

The Red Cross and other agencies offer some medical help to the urban poor in India and Bangladesh

Megacities

One striking result of the high rates of natural increase in urban populations has been the emergence of **megacities**, cities with populations of 10 million people or more. In 1960, New York and Tokyo were the only cities with 10 million or more inhabitants. Today there are 17 such megacities. These include Beijing, Cairo, Calcutta, Jakarta, Lagos, Manila, Mexico City, Sao Paulo, Shanghai and Tehran. By 2015 there are expected to be 26 megacities: 22 in less-developed regions, 18 of them in Asia.

Rio de Janeiro is a megacity. There are expected to be 26 megacities (cities with populations of 10 million or more) by 2015.

In which countries are the cities mentioned in the text?

Shanty Towns

Another consequence of **urban population growth** in developing countries has been that many cities have grown **more rapidly than the jobs and housing they can support**. This is called over-urbanisation and it produces instant slums, called **shanties**. It is these slums and squatter settlements that must absorb the unprecedented rates of urban growth in the megacities of the developing world.

Squatter settlements are not necessarily slums, but most are. They have many names, such as **favelas** in Brazil and **bustees** in India.

> Over-urbanisation occurs when migrants are driven from rural areas to large cities where slow economic growth does not provide sufficient jobs or shelter for them.

Child Workers

Over-urbanisation is causing acute problems throughout the less developed world. A 1995 UNICEF report blamed 'uncontrollable urbanisation' in less developed countries for the widespread creation of 'danger zones' where increasing numbers of children are forced to become beggars, prostitutes and labourers before they reach their teens. Pointing out that urban populations are growing at twice the general population growth rate, the report concluded that too many people are being squeezed into cities that do not have the jobs, housing or schools to accommodate them. As a consequence, the family and community structures that support children are being destroyed. The result is that more and more young children have to work to survive.

> What is UNICEF and what does it do?

Male/Female Imbalance

In areas of out-migration in less developed countries, it is the young males who migrate to cities, leaving the female members, including wives, in the rural communities to tend the family's portion of land. The male migrants are urban dwellers loyal to a rural home and so are drawn back from time to time by community obligations.

> Trocaire has a video on the topic of child labour.

IMPACTS OF RURAL TO URBAN MIGRATION IN DEVELOPED COUNTRIES

Urban Sprawl

The migration of rural people to towns and cities has been happening in Europe on a large scale since the Industrial Revolution, about 1750. This occurred because of the creation of industrial jobs on coalfield sites. However, urban sprawl and the spreading of cities out into the countryside was really a twentieth-century phenomenon in developed countries. It consists mainly of **large housing estate developments on the edges of cities**. The demand for spacious houses with front and rear gardens creates this urban growth problem. The quality of these houses is in stark contrast to the shanty developments on the outskirts of cities in less developed countries.

Urban sprawl spreads across the Nevada Desert

The spreading of cities out into the countryside is a global problem, but in the developed world it is happening at increasing speed. Sprawl is understandable, maybe unavoidable, in countries where the population is growing rapidly. But it is more difficult to explain in developed countries with much lower birth rates. In some regions, urban sprawl is growing five times faster than urban populations.

Growth centres

One way to restrict urban sprawl is to create growth boundaries. This leads to the creation of growth centres, such as the development of new towns some distance away from major cities. In the Netherlands, for instance, towns such as Leystad and Almere have been developed to prevent urban sprawl in the Greenheart of the Randstad.

Rural Depopulation

In the developed world the inability of large areas of land (even in excess of 40 hectares in Ireland) to support a family is causing a desire for rural people to migrate to cities to increase their income. This rural/urban movement has created large rural regions of low population density in developed countries. Examples of such areas in the EU are the West of Ireland, the Massif Central in France and the Mezzogiorno in southern Italy.

Did you know that the world's cities take up just 2 per cent of the earth's land surface? Yet they account for 76 per cent of industrial wood use, 60 per cent of the water tapped for human use and 78 per cent of the carbon emissions from human activities, believed by most scientists to be the major cause of global warming.

Rural Areas to Inner City

There's a conscious movement by two categories of people to inner city areas.

- Recent waves of immigration to inner city areas occur due to the low cost and easy availability of accommodation in large cities of, for example, the USA. The immigrants, Hispanics from Mexico, Puerto Ricans and Cubans, Chinese, Filipinos, Japanese and Koreans, cluster within inner city zones and form ethnic zones or ghettos within these large cities. At present large numbers of immigrants are finding accommodation in the Dublin's north inner city. New shops have opened selling products, such as certain foods, to suit the new cultural groups.
- There has been a spectacular growth of financial and business centres in some of the more prestigious cities, such as Dublin's Financial Centre and London's Docklands. In such cities many of the young middle class have turned their backs on the rural-urban movement to the suburbs, and purchase or rent accommodation in urban renewal areas. Such movement is generally by unmarried single people and divorced single people who find easier access to work, entertainment and friends.

Urban renewal has led to the development of many inner city areas such as Limerick City. Many other town developments, such as this one in Dungarvan, have attracted people to waterfront areas.

Counter-Urbanisation

The most recent pattern of internal migration has been an urban to rural movement in well-developed and urbanised countries. Since the 1960s this migration trend has occurred in some individual countries, such as Scotland, England and the Netherlands. But because it is now occurring throughout the western developed world, it is being regarded as a new pattern.

Counter-urbanisation is indirectly an impact of rural to urban migration, and yet is also directly created by rural to urban movement.

Rural to urban migration has created large **conurbations**. These are large areas of urban environment created by the expansion of cities towards each other, such as the Randstad. In other worlds conurbations are created by urban sprawl. Because of traffic jams, rush-hour traffic, limited open space, crime and a **deteriorating quality of life** in some cities, many people who lived in these urban environments have **moved to rural areas**. An additional factor in driving this urban to rural movement is the **high cost of housing in cities**. These high city prices have allowed some people to sell their home in the city, to buy or build a new home in a rural environment and have left-over funds in their bank accounts for family security or other purposes.

Almere was designed to accommodate overspill population from Amsterdam. It is a new town built on reclaimed land in the north-east polder. This photograph suggests that living in Almere would have many advantages.

Daily Rural to Urban Migration

Daily commuting to work from rural to urban areas is mainly associated with developed industrial societies. This occurs especially into cities in the morning, and out from cities in the evening, when people are going to and coming from work. This daily movement leads to rush-hour traffic and causes traffic jams throughout most urban regions of the developed world.

Three factors seem to have created this new trend.
1. Widespread availability of comfort services provided by the state, such as electrification, piped water, well-surfaced and improved roads, and network television. This can only be achieved in wealthy countries with sufficient funds to support populations in rural areas even though it is not economically viable to do so.
2. Improved private income that allows people to choose where they want to live.
3. The trade-off that people make between material things on the one hand and the quality of life and environmental considerations on the other. Quality of life is winning the battle, with people on higher incomes opting for a 'rural' location in peripheral areas.

The recent growth in the Irish economy has led to the development of many houses in rural towns throughout the country.

Rural to Urban Movement in Ireland

The improvements in roads, as well as the slowly improving rail service, has allowed the slowing of rural to urban migration in Ireland. People are now willing to travel much further to work than they were in the 1970s and 1980s. This allows them the choice of remaining in the countryside or moving to a city suburb. In addition, the high cost of housing in urban areas, especially in Dublin and its satellite towns, has been a limiting factor in rural to urban migration. This is leading to a rapid growth in smaller towns and villages throughout the country, where houses or house sites may be purchased at lower cost and, on balance, with a better quality of life for young families.

> Remember, rural to urban migration also continues as before during the process of counter-urbanisation.

Renewal in seaside towns

The inclusion of seaside towns in urban renewal has led to a renewed interest in people making their homes by the sea and commuting to work each day. Seaside 'designated areas' policies have replaced dreary, damp old buildings with new ones that provide modern facilities, such as restaurants, fitness and swimming facilities, hotels and cafes. Some of these seaside towns, such as Cobh in County Cork and Malahide near Dublin, are near large towns and have become attractive to young families as the location for their family home. Many people commute to work each day from these places.

Daily commuting has increased in recent years as a consequence of high house prices in Dublin

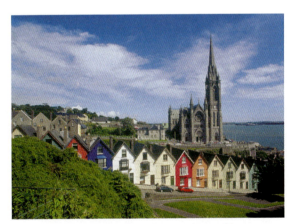

Many large, traditional family houses in seaside towns have been upgraded to modern standards

Skibbereen in Co. Cork

Class activity

Imagine a major Civil Service department with 600 employees is to be transferred from Dublin to this town.

1. Choose a site for the new government building. Then give two advantages of this site for the new structure.
2. Fully explain two ways in which this transfer would affect:
   (a) the structure of the town; (b) the services of the town;
   (c) the social life of the area.
3. Explain two ways in which the transfer might improve the quality of life of the civil servants who move to the town.
4. Explain two ways in which the transfer could negatively affect their quality of life.

SECTION 4 (CHAPTERS 9–14)
THE DYNAMICS OF SETTLEMENT

 **KEY IDEA!** Settlements can be identified in relation to site, situation and function.

This section examines the historical development of towns in Ireland. It looks at how urban growth over time has led to changes in size, land use, functions and residential segregation. It also examines rural settlement patterns and how new planning strategies in rural areas may influence future housing developments.

- Chapter 9 Site Characteristics of Villages, Towns and Cities
- Chapter 10 Locational Characteristics of Ireland's Prehistoric and Historic Settlements
- Chapter 11 Rural Settlement Patterns
- Chapter 12 Planning Strategies in Rural Areas
- Chapter 13 Urban Hierarchy, Hinterland and Central Place Theory
- Chapter 14 The Functions and Services of Settlements Change Over Time

Some older areas of cities fall into decay

Retail parks act as growth centres in urban regions

Some major cities' rapid transport systems help them to remain dynamic

63

CHAPTER 9
SITE CHARACTERISTICS OF VILLAGES, TOWNS AND CITIES

SITE AND SITUATION OF SETTLEMENTS

Function refers to the activities of a settlement, such as a seaside resort, market town, or other commercial and industrial activities. As settlements grow they add more and more functions. Some towns are classified by their main function, such as fishing port.

Site refers to the characteristics of the actual ground or point at which the settlement is located, and was of major importance in the initial development and growth of the village or town. **Situation** refers to the location of the village or town relative to its surroundings, such as neighbouring settlements, rivers and uplands. For example, Athlone is sited at a bridging point of the river Shannon. It is situated in County Westmeath on the Central Plain of Ireland. The combined description of site and situation is called the **location** of a settlement. Situation as well as human and political factors determined whether or not a particular settlement remained small or grew into a larger town or city.

Early settlements in Ireland developed in a rural economy and aimed at being self-sufficient, mainly because transport was limited at that time. The most important factors that determined the site of a settlement are shown in Figure 9.1 and are described below. However, it is important to note that several of these factors would have combined when a choice was being made in the siting of a settlement.

The most import factors are:

- **Water supply.** A nearby, constant clean water supply was essential for everyday needs. Water is heavy and difficult to carry. Until the 1950s most rural villages and homes relied on a village pump or well for their water supply. In earlier times, rivers were sufficiently clean to provide clean drinking water. In hillside areas many villages and farmhouses were located near a spring or well.

Fig. 9.1 Factors that determine the site of a settlement

- **Avoidance of flooding.** By their very nature many parts of river flood plains are covered by water during times of heavy rain. Because of this only dry sites at selected fording (shallow) points of rivers were chosen for town development. Other, more low-lying areas were avoided for all settlement.

- **Food supply.** Towns and villages were generally built in gently sloping fertile areas where food could be produced from grazing of animals or tillage. Consequently, all Irish urban settlements are in lowland areas.

SITE CHARACTERISTICS OF VILLAGES, TOWNS AND CITIES

- **Defence, bridging points and nodal sites.** Some sites are of strategic importance, such as bridging points of rivers and harbour entrances. Routes focus on and meet at these places. In historic times, castles were built at such places to defend these sites.
- **Resources.** Settlements also grew in places where there were natural resources, such as minerals, e.g. Silvermines Village in County Tipperary, or at mineral springs, such as Lisdoonvarna in County Clare.
- **Harbours and seaside resorts.** Sheltered harbours and bays provided suitable sites for the development of settlements. As ships became larger some ports lost their importance as they were not deep enough to accommodate these vessels.

Case Study: location of Skibbereen – sample answer

Site. Skibbereen is sited on the left bank (south side) of the Llen River. The town is sited on sloping land between 5 and 40 metres above sea level. The western side slopes steeply towards the river while the eastern side is built on more gently sloping and level ground. It is sited on the left bank to avoid the low-lying flat land on the right bank. This flat area forms part of the flood plain of the River Llen. The word 'marsh' suggests this is true. This site was chosen because of its elevated site and because it was a suitable bridging point of the river.

Situation. Skibbereen is located in the valley of the Llen River, which runs north-east to south-west across a low-lying hilly landscape. It is located at the junction of major routes across the lowland. The R593, R596, R637, R595 and the N71 and some third-class roads all meet at Skibbereen. Skibbereen is a bridging point of the Llen River and so Skibbereen is a major route focus.

In which direction was the camera pointing when this photograph was taken?

THE DYNAMICS OF SETTLEMENT

Remember the Donegal region in the physical section of *Our Dynamic World 1*. (The trend of the Donegal uplands.)

Class activity

Carefully study the Ordnance Survey map of Letterkenny.

1. Describe the location (site and situation) of Letterkenny.
2. Suggest how the site of Letterkenny has influenced the shape of the town.
3. Explain how its site has influenced the road network in the regions.
4. Explain how the flood plain of the River Swilly has influenced (a) the siting of houses; (b) the siting of routes.

SITE CHARACTERISTICS OF VILLAGES, TOWNS AND CITIES

Class activity
Carefully study the photograph of Enniskillen above.
1. How has the site of Enniskillen influenced the shape of the town? In your answer refer to (a) the town centre and (b) the suburbs.
2. What advantages has this site as a centre for urban development?
3. Are the housing estates well planned or poorly planned developments? Explain.
4. Identify the types of dwellings located in the centre foreground of the photograph.

CHAPTER 10
LOCATIONAL CHARACTERISTICS OF IRELAND'S PREHISTORIC AND HISTORIC SETTLEMENTS

SITE, SITUATION AND FUNCTION OF IRELAND'S PREHISTORIC SETTLEMENTS

Ireland's First Settlements

The earliest settlers came to Ireland about 9,000 years ago (around 7000 B.C.). They were **hunters, fisherfolk** and **food-gatherers**. They were Mesolithic people, which means they belonged to the Middle Stone Age. However, the earliest evidence of these people – midden sites, called 'Midden' on Ordnance Survey maps – dates from about 5,000 years ago. Midden sites are mounds of sand with bones of wild pig and deer as well as heaps of empty seashells. These midden sites are **sited near today's shoreline**, just **above high tide level**. Many of them are also **covered by sand dunes** that formed by wind and wave action after they were abandoned. Middens represent temporary settling places where people lived and hunted and gathered berries and shellfish.

> What were the functions of **middens**? Why did their location suit their function?

Class activity
1. Locate each midden site on the map extract using six-figure grid references.
2. Describe the general locational characteristics of these middens. (Where are they and why are they located here?)

Ireland's First Farming Settlements

Farming was first practised in Ireland about 7,000 years ago (5000 B.C.). These farming people belonged to the Neolithic or New Stone Age and they chose sites for their homes in places where cattle could be raised and some grain could be grown successfully. They chose **upland areas** and **raised, dry or hilly lowland** sites for their farms and tilled the surrounding land. Soils were rich in lime at that time and the upland soils were lighter (grittier) and easy to work with primitive wooden farming tools.

Three regions were of particular importance:
- **The Burren**. Early farmers grazed cattle and grew crops in this region.
- **The lowland drumlin soils of Sligo to Dundalk** provided rich grazing.
- **West Cork**, where copper ore for smelting was available.

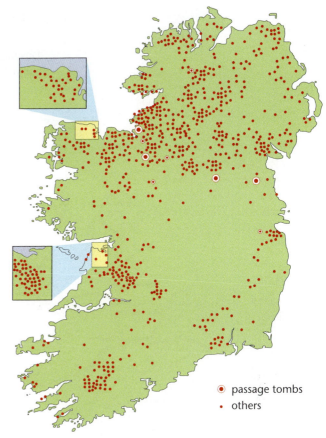

Fig. 10.1 Ireland's megalithic tombs

Neolithic people lived on their farmland and buried their dead in large stone tombs called **megaliths**. While little evidence of their homes remains, the site and situation of their tombs indicate the places where they lived and worked. Their tombs form a **dispersed pattern** across these regions, many of them in elevated areas. Later farming groups came during the Copper and Bronze ages (2000–650 B.C.) and many of these groups also chose elevated sites to live, worship and bury their dead. Descriptions such as **Stone Circle**, **Barrow**, **Cairns**, **Cist**, **Standing Stones** and **Fulachtai Fiadh** (all printed in red on Ordnance Survey maps) indicate the sites of these later farming groups.

Celtic Settlements

From about 650 B.C. to A.D. 250 numerous groups of people who introduced a new culture migrated to Ireland. These newcomers were the Celts. The Celts had a structured society that included royal families, druids, judges, freemen and farmers. They lived in communities, some large and some small, **throughout farming lowland**. They also divided the country into divisions called Tuaths.

Structures such as hill forts, ring forts, crannogs, cashels and promontory forts are associated with the

Stone circles were places of religious worship during the Stone Age in Ireland

THE DYNAMICS OF SETTLEMENT

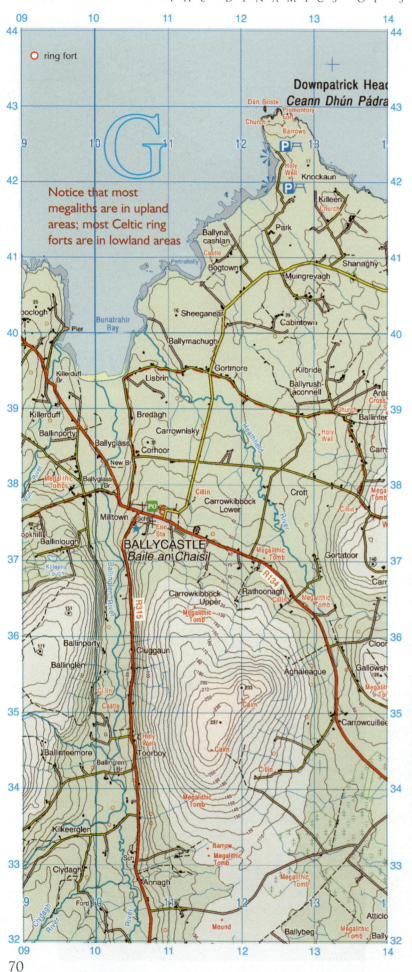

Celts. Promontory forts were built on cliff edges for protection against attack. Forts were mostly circular in shape and their use varied from house enclosures to animal shelters, ceremonial sites and defence. **Elevated sites**, such as **hilltops** or **cliff edges**, were regularly chosen for the largest of these structures.

Celtic settlements may be identified by names such as Rath (Rathluirc), Lios (Lisdoonvarna), Dun (Dundalk), Caher (Cahir), Cashel (Cashel). Folklore referred to some of these settlements as fairy forts.

Class activity
Carefully study the Ordnance Survey map.
1. Identify, and explain the reason for, the pattern in the site and situation of early Stone Age burial sites in this area.
2. Identify and explain the pattern in the site and situation of Celtic ring forts in this area.
3. State how the function of these settlements is suited to their site and situation.

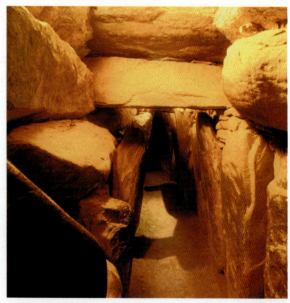

Passage tombs such as Newgrange are among our most important Stone Age burial sites

Prehistoric settlements near Ballycastle, County Mayo

LOCATIONAL CHARACTERISTICS OF IRELAND'S PREHISTORIC AND HISTORIC SETTLEMENTS

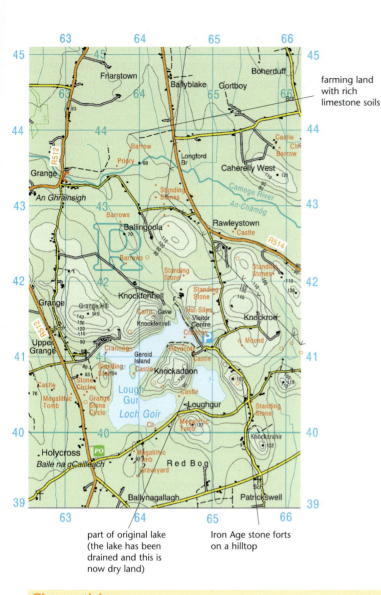

- farming land with rich limestone soils
- part of original lake (the lake has been drained and this is now dry land)
- Iron Age stone forts on a hilltop

A royal ceremonial hill fort at the Hill of Tara.

Dun Aengus is a stone promontory fort on a cliff in the Aran Islands

Class activity

The Lough Gur area has had continuous settlement since early farming times. *Using evidence from the map only, suggest why Knockadoon hill was a suitable location for early settlement.*

Circular stone forts were called 'cashel' or 'caher'

The Celts established a network of routeways throughout Ireland. In wet and marshy areas they built roads, called **toghers**, from planks of wood on brushwood.

71

THE DYNAMICS OF SETTLEMENT

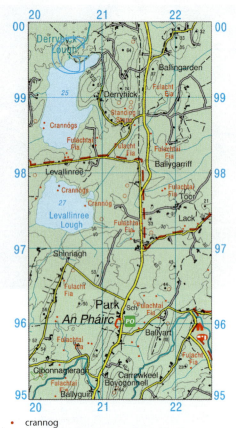

- crannog
○ ring fort

Class activity
Carefully study the photographs on the previous page and the Ordnance Survey maps here and on the previous page.
1. A fulacht fia was a cooking place in the Bronze Age. How does the pattern of their locations on these maps reflect their function?
2. Describe the site and situation of the three crannogs in Levallinree Lake. Why does this location suit the function/activity of these settlements?
3. Many groups of prehistoric and historic peoples settled around Lough Gur in County Limerick (page 71). Identify these different groups and say why this location was suited to the needs/activities of so many different settlement groups in the past. (Hint: water, fowl, fish, defence.)

> Crannogs were sometimes used as settlement sites or as cattle enclosures. They were man-made islands in lakes and were built for protection.

Small Hermit Monasteries

Sites chosen by early missionaries were in **scattered, isolated scenic areas**. Generally they were in **glaciated valleys**. The peace and rugged natural beauty of the surrounding land formed an integral part of early monastic life. It was a simple life **located away from people** where the monks could feel near to God. These monks were called **hermits**. Some of them lived in small 'bee-hive' huts built of stone. Most, however, lived in thatched timbered buildings that have since decayed. Nearby was their **church**, often a small stone building, where they worshipped.

A local stream, lake or spring provided an unpolluted supply of fresh water. At that time rivers had enormous quantities of trout and salmon throughout the year. Some food crops were grown nearby on fertile ground.

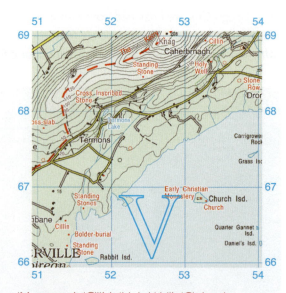

'Monastery', 'Cillín', 'Holy Well', 'Ch.' and 'Cross-inscribed Stone' indicate early Christian monastic settlements

LOCATIONAL CHARACTERISTICS OF IRELAND'S PREHISTORIC AND HISTORIC SETTLEMENTS

SITE, SITUATION AND FUNCTION IN THE HISTORIC DEVELOPMENT OF IRISH TOWNS

Large Monastery Settlements

Monasteries were built:

- **At route centres**, such as Clonmacnoise in County Offaly.
- **On fertile plains and river valleys**, such as Kells, in County Meath, and Kilkenny City.

Some monasteries grew into substantial settlements that became centres of education for people in Ireland, Britain and the European continent at a time when such schools were not available elsewhere. At the centre was the monastery with its church or churches, round tower, monks' dwellings and graveyard, all of which were enclosed by a circular stone wall.

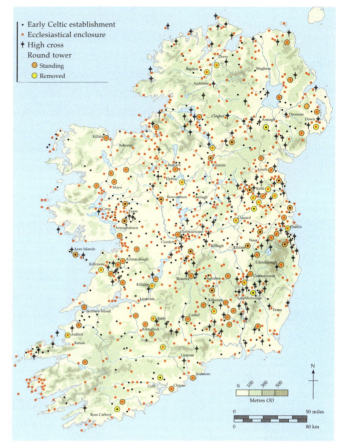

Fig. 10.2 The locations of early Irish monasteries

Place names can help to identify some early Christian monastic settlements. The words **'Manistir'**, **'Cill'** or **'Ceall'** mean a church, so settlements whose names begin with any of these words may have monastic origins. Examples include Kilkenny, Kilbride and Monasterevin. As these towns grew, they developed functions other than religious and educational, such as metal working and other trades.

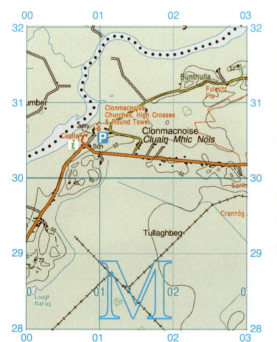

Clonmacnoise, County Offaly

Some early monasteries are identifiable from the air. They are small stone buildings with steep roofs or gables. A circular wall around the monastery can sometimes still be seen. Later monasteries had round towers. These were tall, circular, tapering stone towers built to protect their occupants against attack.

THE DYNAMICS OF SETTLEMENT

To recap, look at the ESB video on the Shannon Basin. Then focus on the part dealing with Clonmacnoise.

Class activity
Carefully study the Ordnance Survey map and photograph on the previous page.
1. Identify the settlement in the photograph.
2. Describe the site, situation and function of this settlement.
3. Explain why this site and situation was suited to the function of the settlement. One of your points should refer to transport. Use evidence from the photograph and Ordnance Survey map only.
4. Some monastic settlements that began at this time in Ireland have survived and are thriving towns today. Suggest one fully developed reason why this settlement failed to survive.

Fig. 10.3

Class activity
Study Fig. 10.3. Then identify the Viking towns numbered 1–8 and the other towns, 9–16.
'All these settlements share a common site and function.'
Explain this statement.

Viking Settlements

The Vikings first came to Ireland in the late eighth century and established our first formal towns on coastal estuaries. These settlements were built on defensive sites at waterside locations that also acted as **trading bases** or **ports for trade** between Ireland, Britain and continental Europe. These **sheltered river estuaries** provided safe anchorage for the Viking longboats.

Norman and Medieval Settlements

The Normans came to Ireland in 1169 and landed at Bannow Bay in County Wexford. From there they spread west and north, capturing the best farmland and setting up castles to defend their captured land.

The Normans were particularly good at choosing **defensive sites** and most of their settlements have survived and developed into Ireland's most prosperous cities and towns. The Normans often chose sites for their mottes and castles where there were already thriving monastery settlements, such as Clonmacnoise, Roscrea and Kilkenny. In most cases, however, they chose new sites that were easily defended, such as **bridging points**, **river loops**, **elevated sites** or **islands** in rivers. For example, Cahir Castle in County Tipperary is sited on an island in the River Suir. Sometimes their first building was a motte and bailey. On other occasions it was a stone castle.

Unplanned towns developed around these defensive buildings, which provided protection for the townsfolk and soldiers. These towns grew by **adding buildings and functions**, such as abbeys. The towns were surrounded by high walls and their guarded gateways were the only ways of entering or leaving the settlements. The larger the settlement the more gateways it had.

Cahir Castle was built on an island in the River Suir

Other functions of Norman towns

The Normans, who were Christian, encouraged religious orders such as the Cistercians and Franciscans to establish monasteries here, so these religious buildings, called **abbeys**, are often found **near Norman castles** throughout the south and east, where most Norman towns are found. These abbeys are generally sited **near rivers** as fish formed a large part of the monks' diet. Monastic lands near the towns were called **granges**.

During the Middle Ages, these abbeys performed a number of functions. They frequently provided **alms** for the poor, **education** for the young, **accommodation** for travellers and **hospitals** for the ill. The abbeys also created **urban growth** by increasing trade. They created markets within Ireland and abroad for cattle, horses and wool. These activities helped the Norman towns to grow into **market centres** where **fairs** and **markets** were held regularly. Industries such as **milling** and **tanning** leather associated with market towns also developed. Because of these developments Norman towns thrived and survive as our main towns today.

Some towns, such as Ennis in County Clare, developed around abbeys. Can you identify the abbey in this photograph?

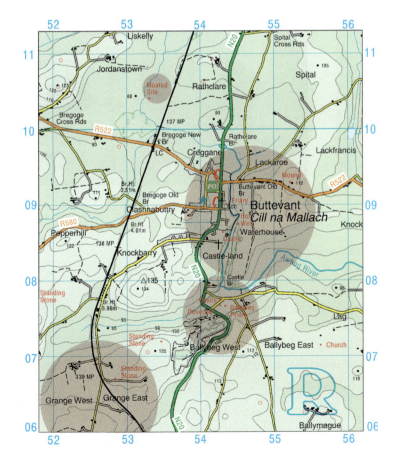

Class activity
Carefully study the photograph of Ennis above.
1. Explain why this town developed at this location.
2. What evidence in the town's plan/layout suggests it had a medieval origin? Explain.

Class activity
Carefully study the Ordnance Survey map of Buttevant in County Cork.
1. Who, in your opinion, chose this site for a settlement? Explain fully.
2. Describe the site, situation and original functions of this settlement.
3. Explain two factors that were important originally in the town's location and still contribute to the settlement's survival today. Use evidence from the map to support your answer.

Recognising castles and abbeys in aerial photographs

Generally, today's dwellings, commercial offices and other buildings have either a brick or plaster finish. Some share similar characteristics. In Norman times, castles and abbeys also had common characteristics. They were built of stone and had tower-like features. Look for these structures on a map or photograph to identify a town's origins. Norman and medieval towns were unplanned settlements.

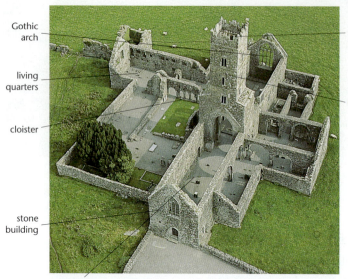

St Mary's Cathedral in Limerick is of Norman origin

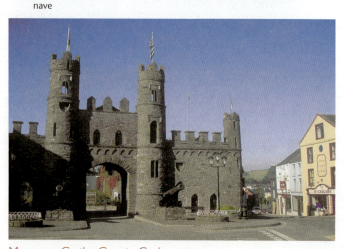

Macroom Castle, County Cork

Dalkey Castle, County Dublin

Abbeys had Gothic style architecture, with pointed windows and doorways. Like castles, they were built of stone. They also had bell towers that resembled castles.

The presence of an abbey tells us three things about a town:
- It was a Norman town.
- The abbey had many functions in the daily life of the settlement.
- Abbeys were closed down in the sixteenth century as towns lost some of their functions.

Class activity
Can you identify the functions of the buildings in these photographs?

LOCATIONAL CHARACTERISTICS OF IRELAND'S PREHISTORIC AND HISTORIC SETTLEMENTS

Kinsale, County Cork, showing evidence of its medieval origins: irregular streets; no obvious planning; streets meet at irregular angles where markets were held

Kinsale in County Cork is one of Ireland's best known medieval towns. Study these characteristics so that you will recognise them in parts of other towns.

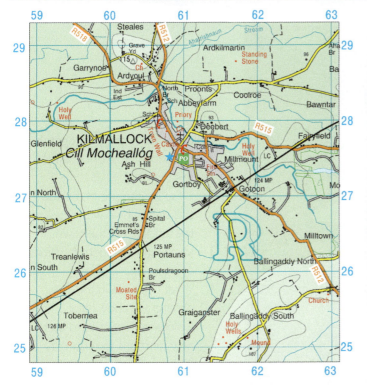

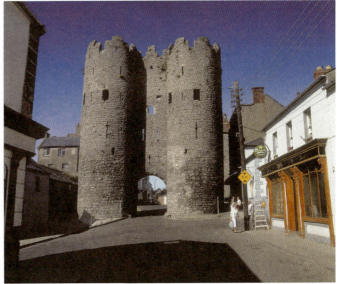

Gates, such as St Lawrence's Gate in Drogheda, controlled entry to medieval towns

Class activity
Carefully study the Ordnance Survey map of Kilmallock in County Limerick.
1. Describe the site of the town.
2. Explain the origin of the town. (Hint: place name.)
3. Explain the second and further stages in the town's development (functions). Use evidence from the map to support your points.

77

Planned Plantation Towns and Villages

Planned towns and villages were built as part of the plantations of the sixteenth and seventeenth centuries. The earliest planned towns and villages, such as Portlaoise and Birr, are located in **Laois** and **Offaly**. Other plantation towns were located in Munster, including Youghal, Mallow and Bandon in County Cork. All these Munster towns have a few parallel, narrow main streets. Most plantation towns, however, such as Donegal, Cavan, Monaghan and Clones, are located in **Ulster** and were built on greenfield sites after the Ulster Plantation of 1609.

The main functions of plantation settlements

Plantation towns and villages had a number of functions. These included:
- To defend settlers against attack from dispossessed Irish farmers by enclosing the towns with defensive walls.
- To encourage settlers to come to Ireland.
- To create business and wealth by building market squares and fair greens to accommodate farm animals and market stalls on market and fair days.
- To introduce the Protestant faith by building new churches.
- To provide homes for business people and other traders and workers.

Coleraine, a planned town in Co. Derry

> **Class activity**
> **Carefully study the photograph.**
> 1. Describe the layout (plan) of this town.
> 2. Describe the site of the town and state why it was suited to the functions of the town.
> 3. Identify two modern functions of the town.
> 4. What evidence in the photograph shows that Coleraine continues to add new functions to ensure its future survival?

Many of Ireland's villages were built in the eighteenth and nineteenth centuries. Some of them, such as Birr in County Offaly, grew into towns. These settlements were **planned** and some, such as Durrow in County Offaly, had a **square** or **green**. Their **streets** were **wide** and well planned. They had fine and graceful buildings, some of which were shops, while others were erected as town dwellings for the country gentry, merchants and army officers. Many were two, three or four storeys in height.

Most of these planned towns were **located next to a large estate, castle or demesne** that was owned by the local landlord on whose land the town was built. He often took a special interest in the layout of the settlement that gave it its own unique character.

> **Class activity**
> Carefully study the photograph of Kilrush, County Clare.
> 1. What evidence in the photograph suggests that this town was a planned settlement?
> 2. What advantages does the planned layout of this town offer today's planners in helping to cope with traffic flow within the town?

Kilrush, a planned town in County Clare

Ireland's Coastal Cities and Towns

Ireland's largest coastal settlements are sited at the lowest bridging points of rivers before they enter the sea. As such they were **defensive sites** that could control our deepest sheltered harbours and were the **meeting points of inland and coastal routeways**. They were all either Viking, Norman or plantation defensive towns that served large fertile hinterlands, so they also had **market functions**. Over the centuries they added new functions to provide services for each town and their trade areas. These functions included **port functions, milling, brewing, manufacturing, law, education (universities), recreation, cultural, religious** and **administrative**. Some large coastal cities and towns include Dublin, Cork, Limerick, Galway (cities), Wicklow, Wexford, Dingle and Sligo (towns).

Small villages and towns also developed as fishing and recreational centres, such as Dunfanaghy in County Donegal

THE DYNAMICS OF SETTLEMENT

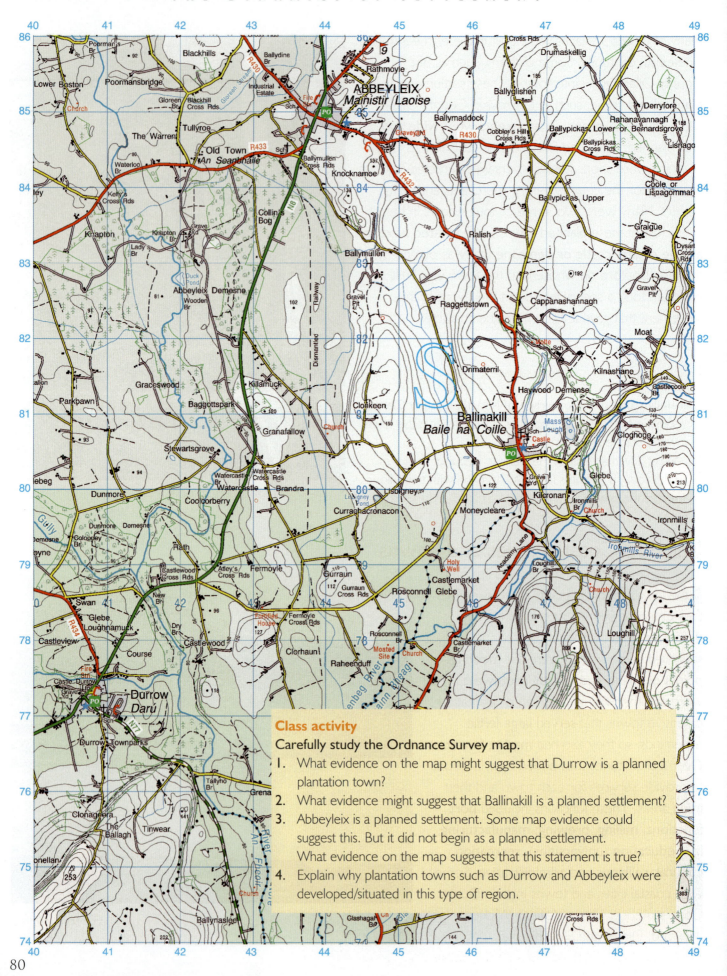

Class activity

Carefully study the Ordnance Survey map.

1. What evidence on the map might suggest that Durrow is a planned plantation town?
2. What evidence might suggest that Ballinakill is a planned settlement?
3. Abbeyleix is a planned settlement. Some map evidence could suggest this. But it did not begin as a planned settlement. What evidence on the map suggests that this statement is true?
4. Explain why plantation towns such as Durrow and Abbeyleix were developed/situated in this type of region.

Industrial and Town Growth in the Eighteenth and Nineteenth Centuries

Canal towns

Some of Ireland's largest rivers, such as the Shannon, the Liffey, the Erne and the Barrow were deepened, widened and connected by canals during the eighteenth and nineteenth centuries. This allowed barges to carry **heavy and bulky goods** from our largest coastal ports to inland towns that were already sited on rivers. In addition they now found themselves sited on **canals**. These inland towns, such as Athy, Carlow, Athlone and Carrick-on-Shannon, became river ports that catered for the transport of **people** and **goods**, such as grain and timber brought from the hinterlands of inland canal towns to the coast for export. They also catered for the transport of goods, such as beer and coal, from coastal ports to inland areas. All this cargo had to be loaded and unloaded by hand and stored on the canal side. So large **grain stores, mills, warehouses** and **hotels** were built on waterside sites in these canal towns. This increased trade, created employment and increased the prosperity of these settlements.

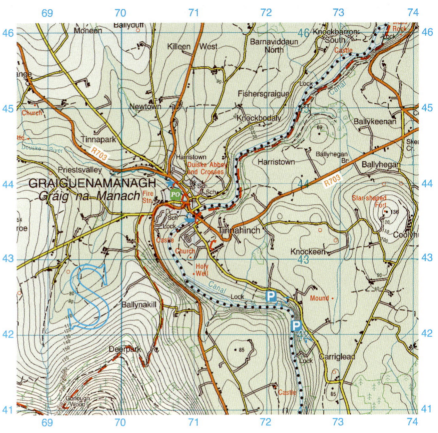

Graiguenamanagh is a port settlement on the River Barrow

Class activity

Carefully study the Ordnance Survey map and the photograph.

1. What evidence along the River Barrow suggests that this river was canalised?
2. Identify a building or buildings directly associated with canal transport. Explain fully.
3. What economic developments in the town would have been encouraged as a consequence of the canal?

Locks were built on rivers to allow the controlled raising and lowering of water levels to accommodate barge movement.

Class activity

1. Identify the various categories of Irish towns that you have studied so far.
2. Give a brief account as to where each category of town is located.
3. Explain why each category is sited at these locations.
4. Identify the common characteristics of most Ulster towns.
5. Why do the structure of Irish towns in the south and east generally differ from the structure of those in Ulster?

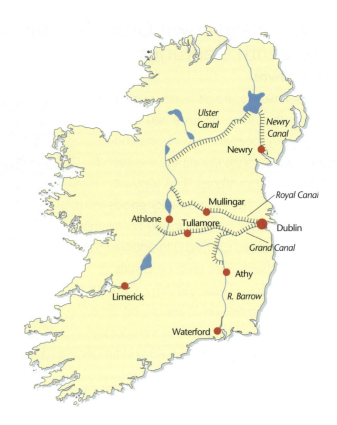

Fig. 10.4 Ireland's canals and canal towns

Lockes Distillery, County Westmeath

Mills

Mills flourished in Ireland during the eighteenth and early nineteenth centuries. These mills represent the equivalent of our modern industries, except they used the energy of fast-flowing water to turn the mill wheels that powered their machines. A sufficient and fast flow of water was generated by building a weir (low dam) across a river to divert some of the flow into a narrow channel called a **race** that rotated the millwheel. Many of these weirs are still present today in rivers that flow through our towns.

Mills were built in many villages and towns throughout Ireland. In Ulster they manufactured linen and wool and milled grain for flour, while in the south they mainly specialised in grain for flour and wool for textiles.

Class activity
These grain stores in New Ross had waterside locations for the storage of goods transported on canals. Identify the characteristics of the grain store in this photograph.

Grain was stored in large warehouses, called granaries, in canal towns. Like industrial buildings at the time they were built of stone, narrow, four or five storeys high, with rows of small windows on each floor level to prevent fires from dust igniting. There were almost 2,000 granaries and mills in Ireland run by landlords or merchants for the export market.

Class activity
Study the map of Letterkenny on page 66. Then explain why the site at C124 091 was suitable for corn and flax mills.

Flax is a plant grown for its fibres, which are used to make linen.

Ireland's Railway Towns
Inland railway towns

Some inland towns that were fortunate enough to be sited on railways achieved increased economic growth in the **nineteenth century**. These towns grew because of increased trade in goods and passenger services. **Hotels** were built **near railway stations** for overnight accommodation. Towns such as Thurles, Portarlington, Mullingar, Athlone and Mallow boomed as cattle were transported from fairs to processing factories, ports and cattle-rearing areas.

Railways helped to speed up the delivery of goods: cargoes that had taken three days for delivery by canal could now be delivered by rail in 10 hours.

Today, the railway is beginning to regain some lost business. Traffic congestion on roads leading into our main towns and cities and the high cost of suburban family homes are encouraging many people to travel by train once again. This has led to a revival of some of our railway stations that are sited on main lines in towns leading to Dublin. Commuting by train is quite common and many find it a much easier and more comfortable way to travel to work than coping with the stress of traffic jams on our roads.

THE DYNAMICS OF SETTLEMENT

Seaside towns

Some seaside towns grew as **railways** were built that **joined them to nearby cities** and towns. Weekend railway trips to the seaside boosted those coastal settlements that were planned with new streets and hotels to accommodate tourists. These seaside towns were **sited near beaches** and **developed around bays** with two- and three-storey buildings that faced out over the beaches towards the sea. Bray in County Wicklow and Tramore in County Waterford grew at this time.

Fig. 10.5 Many buildings in seaside towns have features like bay windows and plaster details. These houses were built at the end of the nineteenth century.

The railways to some of these seaside towns have been dismantled since the 1950s due to the rise in car ownership.

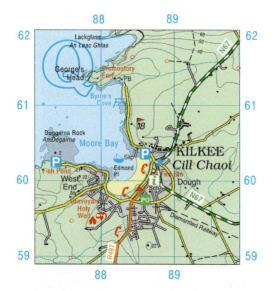

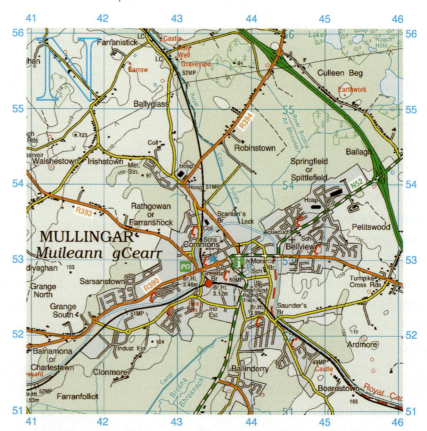

Class activity
Carefully study the Ordnance Survey map of Kilkee.
1. What evidence on the map suggests that the railway once played an active part in the development of the town?
2. What does this suggest about the historical development of Kilkee?

Class activity
Carefully study the Ordnance Survey map of Mullingar. Use evidence from this map to explain the historical development of Mullingar. In your answer refer to canals, railway and roads and other modern developments.

LOCATIONAL CHARACTERISTICS OF IRELAND'S PREHISTORIC AND HISTORIC SETTLEMENTS

Expansion of Ireland's Large Cities and Towns

Most urban rebuilding and development took place during the **Georgian period** (1714–1830). The architectural style, Georgian, takes its name from the four Georges, the English kings who ruled during this period.

In Dublin, Cork, Limerick and Galway suburbs were added to the cities. The older parts of the cities became run down and some developed into **slum areas**.

The new Georgian suburbs had **wide streets with blocks of buildings** and **squares or parks** for the wealthy property owners who lived in their large **four-storey, red-brick terraced** mansions. The streets were wide to cater for horse-drawn carriages and carts for delivering goods. These wide streets reflected **a time of wealth and prosperity** and they differed from the narrow and unplanned older areas of a city. Today, these **Georgian suburbs form the city centre areas of all our largest cities**. Many terraced mansions have been changed into flats. Others have been renovated and are used as offices for insurance companies, solicitors and private business. Some of these terraced mansions overlook Stephen's Green and Merrion Square in Dublin.

A Georgian residence

New towns

New towns, such as **Shannon New Town** and **Tallaght**, were built since the 1960s. Shannon was built to meet the needs of people working in Shannon's industrial estate and airport. Tallaght and Blanchardstown in Dublin were built to cater for the surge in Dublin's population as a consequence of rural to urban migration and movement from Dublin's inner city to the suburbs. A ring of rapidly growing towns has now developed around the city to create the urban region known as Greater Dublin.

Large Gothic-style churches like this one in Cobh were built in the nineteenth century

Traditional eighteenth- and nineteenth-century shopfronts can be seen in many of Ireland's cities and towns

Classical (public) style for courthouses and banks reflected the power of law and finance in society

CHAPTER 11
Rural Settlement Patterns

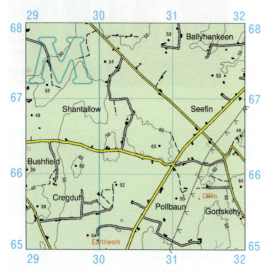
Dispersed (scattered) rural settlements

Clustered rural farm settlements

Rural settlement patterns can be divided into three categories:
- Dispersed.
- Clustered.
- Ribbon development.

DISPERSED SETTLEMENT

Dispersed or scattered housing patterns initially developed when land was 'enclosed' and farms were created from commonage in the eighteenth century. Each farmer built a farmhouse on his own land, which was a change from the medieval village pattern that you studied in your Junior Certificate history course. This gave rise to widely separated houses, especially in the east and south of Ireland, where farms were large. In the west and north-west of Ireland, where farms or plots of land were small, farmhouses were still dispersed but were more closely spaced. Many farmhouses throughout the country were located at the end of long passageways or on roadside sites.

Since the 1960s, many single-storey, two-storey, and dormer-style houses have been built by non-farming people on scattered roadside sites. In such cases, the owners either availed of sites that farm owners willingly sold or gave to family members. Such one-off housing is regarded as unsustainable development by some county councils. They fear two possible negative effects in the future:
- The pollution of ground water supplies through soakage from clogged-up septic tank facilities
- The inability of services to cater for the needs of homeowners when they are old and unable to cater for themselves because they are distant from villages and towns where such services or help may be more readily available.

CLUSTERED SETTLEMENT

Dwellings form a cluster, where:
- Farmhouses were built in clusters. These dwellings may be remnants of the old 'clachan' system where small landholders owned separate parcels of land that surrounded the farm village. This pattern was especially common in the west and north-west of Ireland.

RURAL SETTLEMENT PATTERNS

- In parts of County Kilkenny and County Waterford, where farmhouses were built in clusters rather than on their own individual farms during the plantations.
- At road junctions in isolated rural areas where a shop, church or post office may have developed.

RIBBON SETTLEMENT

Ribbon settlement or ribbon development is relatively recent. It has mainly developed since the 1960s. Individual, one-off houses form a continuous or almost continuous line leading out from villages and small towns for a kilometre or more. Ireland's National Development Plan regards such development as unsustainable development that does not blend with the local landscape and is outside speed limit zones. Such development has occurred up to now because:

- Local planning authorities have granted planning permission in the past.
- Services, such as telephone cables, water supply pipes and electricity lines were readily available nearby.
- Landowners could boost their income for essential needs such as education of their children or a child's inheritance. These roadside sites fetched high prices.
- New shops, filling stations and bed and breakfast accommodation wanted roadside sites on routes leading into and out of villages and towns with ready access to passing traffic so as to survive and prosper as businesses.

A clachan near Buckna in County Antrim

Ribbon settlement is an undesirable pattern and is in conflict with the desires of the National Development Plan

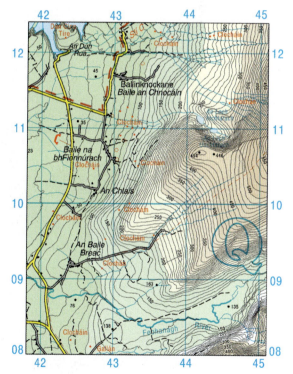

The Irish word *clocháin* refers to rural farming settlements where farmhouses formed a cluster. Most of these houses have been abandoned by their owners.

Class activity
Explain why (a) one-off housing and (b) ribbon settlement are undesirable developments, according to planners.

Clonmel in Co. Tipperary

Class activity

This type of development occurs because of urban expansion. It is urban-generated development.

1. Classify this type of settlement pattern.
2. Explain why this settlement pattern could create hazards:
   (a) for motorists; (b) for local residents.
3. Why might this type of settlement development be classed as undesirable by planners?

CHAPTER 12
Planning Strategies in Rural Areas

COUNTY AND NATIONAL DEVELOPMENT PLANS

Sustainable development is that which seeks an acceptable quality of life for present and future generations. It also recognises that the actions of the present affect the inheritance of future generations and that natural environments must be supported to secure this aim. Sustainable development is the key to managing economic and environmental interdependence.

The way that land is used has a major influence on the type of pressures that are allowed to act on the environment. Those responsible for planning in both rural and urban areas, which involves long periods of time, try to promote the orderly development of the landscape to:

- Ensure the land is used for the common good (the good of everybody).
- Meet the needs of society for housing, food and materials, employment and leisure.
- Support policies concerned with regional development, social integration, urban renewal and the maintenance of strong rural communities.
- Balance competing needs and protect the environment as much as possible.

> Sustainable development is an approach in which the exploitation of resources, the direction of investments, new technological developments and institutional change are made to support future as well as present needs.

Careful planning can help to achieve these objectives in a number of ways:

- Controlling the development of transport, natural resources and the efficient use of energy.
- The careful location of industry, houses and business/shops/services.
- Controlling the shape, size and structure of settlements.
- Effectively using already developed areas.
- Protecting and supporting our natural environment and wildlife habitats, including areas and features of outstanding beauty.
- Accommodating new developments in an environmentally sustainable and sensitive manner.
- Strengthening villages and towns, both socially and economically, in order to improve their potential as growth centres.

Are holiday apartments such as these environmentally friendly? Explain.

89

Scattered one-off houses like these in the West of Ireland are not in keeping with the tradition of the region. Do you agree or disagree with this statement? Explain why.

County councils are **legally bound** (a) to determine the policy for the proper planning and development of cities, towns and other areas and (b) to implement the National Development Plan by:

- Controlling planning and enforcing planning decisions.
- Giving greater recognition to the quality and character of the countryside. Sustainable development of rural areas involves respect for nature and natural systems, conservation of habitats, species and features of ecological interest and the protection of the environment.
- Giving good quality decisions and ensuring public participation, openness and proper enforcement.
- Being responsive to change and reviewing development through a compulsory (statutory) five-year review of their development plans.

Urban-Generated Housing in Rural Areas

Even though many people are migrating from rural areas to towns and cities there is severe pressure on land bordering urban areas for one-off housing to meet the needs of those working in urban areas. This growing demand for housing in the countryside from people working in cities and towns is generally unsustainable because their houses:

- Are away from all facilities that householders need, such as work, shops, schools and entertainment and so large quantities of energy/fuel is used to reach these places.
- Are served by individual septic tanks that may pollute groundwater.
- Spoil city boundaries by creating ribbon settlement.
- Increase roads and transport costs.

Department of the Environment guidelines stress the need to ensure a clear dividing line between urban and rural land use, to help prevent urban sprawl and maintain the rural landscape. Do you feel this has been created by present planning departments?

Environmental Impact Assessment (EIA)

Compulsory environmental impact assessment for major individual developments, such as new roadways, forestry that exceeds 70 hectares and the location of waste material disposal areas (dumps) is now an integral and valuable part of development planning and land use management procedures. In addition, with few exceptions, county councils and urban councils have power to require EIAs for projects that do not reach acceptable levels of agreement or standards if the authority considers that a development would be likely to have significant effects on the environment.

Strategic Environmental Assessment (SEA)

In addition to EIAs, SEAs examine in a general way the policies, plans and programmes of environmental impact assessment.

Class activity
Explain the difference between EIAs and SEAs.

PLANNING STRATEGIES IN RURAL AREAS

> **Class activity**
>
> Carefully study the Ordnance Survey map of part of the Slieve Felim Mountains in County Limerick.
>
> Limerick County Council proposed to create a regional waste disposal area for Limerick, Tipperary and North Cork at grid reference R 788 567. Using evidence from the map, give one reason why such an area may favour such development; and two reasons why the area may not be suited to this development.
>
> If you were the Chief Council Engineer who had the final say in this matter:
> - What steps would you take to ensure your decision was a well-informed one?
> - What would you think a wise outcome would be? Explain.

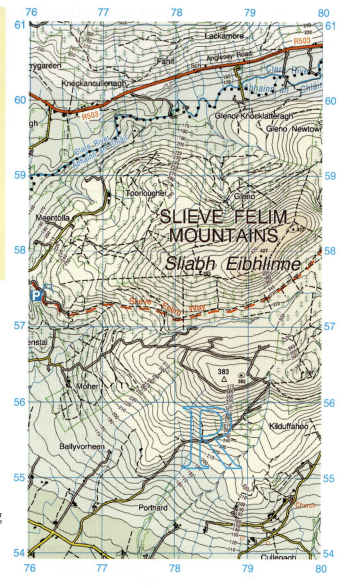

Some Aspects of County Development Plans

One-off housing, such as the dwellings shown on the previous page, is to be restricted as much as possible as these houses are away from many services that people need. They also increase road transport costs to service these sites, such as road widening and re-surfacing of by-roads.

Many argue that such rigid and unsocial planning thinking is flawed. They believe that while new rural housing developments may have economic disadvantages, these considerations are outweighed by the social advantages of rural environments, such as:

- The need for rural communities to be sustained by energetic young people who wish to live and raise families in a rural environment as their parents did.
- A rural environment is cleaner and healthier for young children.
- Rural communities generally have lower crime and substance abuse rates.
- Lower rates of urban sprawl as a consequence of rural development.

> **Class activity**
>
> On page 89 it states that careful planning should control the shape, size and structure of settlements. In the case of each of these factors, suggest measures that must be taken to control the (a) shape (b) size and (c) structures of existing settlements for the common good.

THE DYNAMICS OF SETTLEMENT

Case Study: Oughterard, County Galway

It is desired to achieve self-sustained settlement centres. This is to occur in selected towns and villages. It is to be achieved by encouraging industry, social services, such as health centres (clinics), day-care centres, new small housing estates of just a few houses rather than large developments, the development of existing derelict sites and buildings and the retention of buildings with special characteristics, such as traditional shopfronts.

- Land within settlements, such as towns and villages, is to be zoned for future development, such as housing and industry.
- High-density housing, such as apartments and one- and two-bedroom units, is to be encouraged in settlements so as to cater for people of different ages and income levels.

- Planning permission is to favour **building within existing speed limit areas**. This will over time create a **clear boundary** between villages or towns and the surrounding farmland.
- **Traditional building designs** are to be encouraged rather than the modern, out of character and over-elaborate designs that have been in use since the 1960s.

Class activity
1. Do you agree that the buildings in the photo on the left are in keeping with traditional building designs? Explain.
2. Is high-density housing such as this a positive or negative development in rural villages and towns? Explain.

CHAPTER 13
Urban Hierarchy, Hinterland and Central Place Theory

CLASSIFICATION OF URBAN SETTLEMENTS

Urban settlements can be classified according to size, function and population density. They range in size from the smallest, called a hamlet, through village, small and large town, to small and large city. The small places, such as hamlets and villages, provide for the everyday needs of their residents and those in their immediate vicinity (called hinterland). They have a very limited range of goods and services. The village is likely to have a grocery or general stores, newsagent and sweet shop, public house (bar), filling station, primary school, church and doctor.

Towns have large supermarkets; general clothing, hardware and furniture shops; chemists; jewellers; bookshops; bakeries; secondary schools; dentists; and cinemas. Cities offer more sophisticated shopping and entertainment, so that most people can get all the goods and services they require there. Major department stores, such as Brown Thomas and Marks and Spencer, as well as fashion boutiques, sporting goods and specialist furniture shops, theatres and sports stadiums may be found in cities. Other city services include large hospitals, specialist medical services, universities and cathedrals.

Grafton Street in Dublin. Major towns and cities offer high-order services such as specialised shops and hospitals.

A major function of all urban settlements is to provide services for their inhabitants and the people living in the surrounding areas. The centres, called hamlet, village, town etc., are referred to as central places, because they serve areas larger than themselves. **The nature of central place services and the areas they serve have an important bearing on the arrangement of towns. Central Place Theory** is an attempt to explain the relationship between the **spacing** and the **size** of settlements. However, the idea is based on a flat plain with equal transport in every area and no competition between settlements on shops.

THE DYNAMICS OF SETTLEMENT

Conurbation
A conurbation is an urban area larger than a city. It forms when two cities expand towards each other to create a large urban environment. When two or more conurbations expand and meet they form a megalopolis. Los Angeles is a megalopolis as it is an urban environment formed by the joining of many conurbations. Another megalopolis is in north-east USA where cities from Boston to Washington D.C. create a very extensive urban environment.

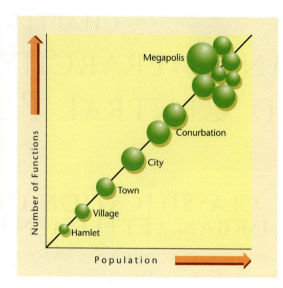

Fig. 13.1 As a settlement's size increases, so does its population and range of services/functions

Are these products low-, medium- or high-order goods?

Three Basic Concepts of Central Place Theory

1. **Range of Goods**. There are low-, middle- and high-order goods and services.
   - **Low-order** goods are those that are required frequently, such as bread, milk, newspapers and petrol. Customers are not prepared to travel very far to obtain such goods.
   - **Middle-order** goods and services, such as large supermarkets, doctors' surgeries and chemists, do not exist in every hamlet or village since they are required less often. So a customer is prepared to travel further for these services than for low-order goods.
   - **High-order** goods are items/services such as furniture, jewellery, law offices, universities, dentists. These goods/services have a high value and are required only occasionally, so customers are willing to travel further for these goods/services than for either low- or middle-order goods/services.

2. **Frequency of demand**. This refers to the level of demand for goods and services, i.e. whether they are required daily, weekly, monthly or yearly. Normally the frequency of demand declines from low- through medium- to high-order goods/services.

3. **Threshold**. Each shop or service has its own market area, and a certain minimum population or threshold population is required before it becomes a viable or financial proposition. A low-order good has a very low threshold population due to its high frequency of demand while a high-order good has a

high threshold population due to its low frequency of demand. It has been suggested that in the United Kingdom, about 300 people are necessary for the success of a village shop, 500 for a primary school, 2500 for a doctor, 25,000 for a shoe shop, 50,000 for a small department store, 60,000 for a large supermarket, 100,000 for a large department store and over 1 million for a university. Services locate where they can maximise the distance from their nearest rival. Such analysis is used by planners for the creation of new towns.

Trade Area or Hinterland

The idea of the area around a town being linked economically and socially to the urban centre (city, town, village or hamlet) is fundamental to Central Place Theory. The area served by a central place (settlement, e.g. city, town etc.) may be called its trade area, but other names may be used, such as **hinterland**, market area or service area. One simple way to define a hinterland would be to ask shopkeepers and other businesses where their customers come from. If these locations were plotted on a local map one would then define the limits of the village's influence, i.e. its hinterland or its trade area.

Why are high-order products available in urban areas such as this?

Central Place Theory describes hinterlands as circular in shape and equal in size but the real situation is not as simple as this. **Hinterlands** may resemble a circular form but they are **regularly distorted** because of the physical landscape. **Barriers**, such as mountain ranges, un-bridged rivers, the coast or a large lake may cause distortion. Political boundaries may have the same effect. On the other hand a good, **well-surfaced, wide roadway** may cause a hinterland to increase lengthways in that direction. This is because people can reach the town quicker and more easily than another settlement that may be closer to their home. Also, the road may connect with another nearby town and so add it to its hinterland.

> A city will have many surrounding towns, villages and townlands as part of its hinterland.

The size of a **hinterland** is partly **dependent** on the size and **functions** of its central place, i.e. settlement, village or town etc. For example, a seaside resort is likely to be smaller than a market town of similar population. This is because the functions of a successful market town are generally far greater then those of a seaside resort. Hinterland size is also affected by **population density**. Larger hinterlands are likely in areas of low population, and people are willing to travel (or have to travel) longer distances for their low-order services. Shops, on the other hand, need to draw people from a long distance in such areas to reach their threshold to survive economically. In recent years An Post attempted to close many of its rural post offices because they were not 'viable economic units'. In other words they were 'not able to pay for themselves'. However, due to political pressure, they remained open. It is quite clear that in recent years small rural villages have lost many of their services because rural depopulation has forced schools, Garda stations, Protestant churches, grocery shops and many more services/functions to close.

THE DYNAMICS OF SETTLEMENT

Class activity

Carefully examine the Ordnance Survey map extract.
1. Why is there an absence of settlement at grid reference areas N 18 33, N 20 32, N 22 32, N 23 30?
2. Will the hinterland (trade area) of Ballycumber need to be smaller or larger in the future to enable it to survive as a central place (in this case a hamlet) as a consequence of the low population density in this region? Explain your answer.
3. In which direction/s is the hinterland of Ballycumber likely to expand? Explain.

Changes in Population Size and Number of Functions

Over the last 50 years there has been a decrease in the number of services available in small settlements and an increase in the number of functions provided by large settlements. This may be due to many factors, for example:

1. Small villages are no longer able to support their former functions (village shop) as the greater wealth and mobility (car ownership) of some rural populations enable them to travel further to larger centres where they can obtain, in a single visit, both high- and low-order goods.

2. Domestic changes (deep freezers, convenience foods) mean that rural householders need no longer make use of daily, low-order services previously available in their village.
3. As larger settlements attract an increasingly larger threshold population, they can increase their variety and number of functions and, by reducing costs (supermarkets), are likely to attract even more customers.
4. In areas experiencing rural depopulation, villages may no longer have a population large enough to maintain existing services.

> **Proposed Fieldwork**
> Why not use Central Place Theory to identify the hinterland of your town or village?
> - Locate a map of your local area that includes all surrounding villages.
> - Identify the various services/functions of your settlement.
> - Create a questionnaire that will identify the distances people are willing to travel for those services/functions.
> - Plot these distances and directions on your local map to identify the hinterland.

The three concepts of range of goods, frequency of demand and threshold control the **size** and **spacing** of central places.

In theory, the maximum hinterland on a featureless plain will be a circle. But this would leave areas between adjoining circles unserved by a central place. To avoid this a pattern of **hexagonals** is drawn to represent the hinterlands of local settlements. This pattern allows the maximum area to be served, minimises travelling distance for the consumers and maximises the number of retail outlets possible.

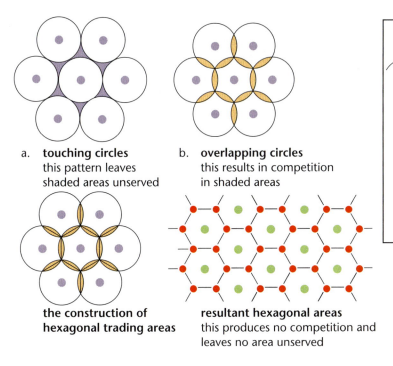

Fig. 13.2

a. **touching circles** this pattern leaves shaded areas unserved
b. **overlapping circles** this results in competition in shaded areas

the construction of hexagonal trading areas

resultant hexagonal areas this produces no competition and leaves no area unserved

Legend:
- central places
- boundary of trade areas
- areas unserved by any central place
- area served by more than one central place
- first-order (lowest) settlement, e.g. village
- second-order settlement, e.g. town

In Junior Certificate geography you studied new settlement patterns on the Dutch polders. You learned that new towns were centrally placed and new villages were planned in a circle around the towns.

Why, with the possible exception of the reclaimed Dutch polders, can no perfect example of Walter Christaller's model be found in the real world? The answer lies in these basic criticisms of central place theory.

> Remember the basic point: the larger the settlement (central place) the greater the area of its hinterland and the more people it serves. A village will serve many individual homes. A town will serve many more homes and many villages. A city will serve large numbers of homes, villages and some towns.

Criticisms of Central Place Theory

- Plains are not featureless or without factors of relief or drainage. Rivers and hills do upset roads.
- Modern transport systems reduce the costs of travel over certain distances, so favouring some centres. These include motorways, tunnels, ferries and railways.
- Population distribution is rarely even and is influenced by transport routes and the location of resources.
- Modern settlements offer a wide range of goods and services, each with its own market. Settlements also compete with each others' neighbouring hinterlands.
- People do not always act rationally. People have preferences in relation to shopping areas. Similarly, traders do not always act on the basis of population statistics when setting up a shop or business.
- Like other models, Central Place Theory is meant as a simplification of reality to help understand the spacing of settlements. It is not meant to be exact. It is useful in regional planning and in market analysis of the trade areas of different shops and their profitability.

> **Class activity**
> Carefully examine the simple exercise in Figure 13.3 and state which town is more likely to expand the most as a consequence of its trade and its hinterland.

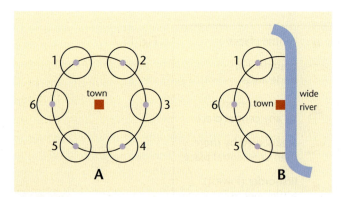

Fig. 13.3 North-east polder in the Netherlands.

> **Class activity**
> Use the concepts of Central Place Theory to do this activity.
> 1. Join the points on each circle to the centrally placed towns A and B.
> 2. What do points 1–6 represent?
> 3. What do the circles around 1–6 represent?
> 4. Which town is likely to be more prosperous, A or B? Explain your answer.

> **Class activity**
> Carefully study the Ordnance Survey map of Nenagh on the opposite page.
> 1. Identify the largest settlement on this map and state what category of settlement it is. For example, is it a city, a town, a village etc.?
> 2. Identify other settlements on the map and state their category/ies.
> 3. List these settlements in terms of their size (called rank size), and in order (called rank order), beginning with the largest.
> 4. Which of these settlements has the smallest hinterland (trade area) and which has the largest? Explain your answers using evidence from the map.
> 5. Which of these settlements would offer low-order services/functions only? Explain fully.
> 6. Which of these settlements would offer low-order and middle-order services? Explain fully.
> 7. At home, write out why Nenagh is a successful urban centre. In your answer, use the concepts that you have learned in this chapter to explain your answer. To help you with the exercise use the following headings: relief and drainage; population density; transport; hinterland (trade area); and services/functions.

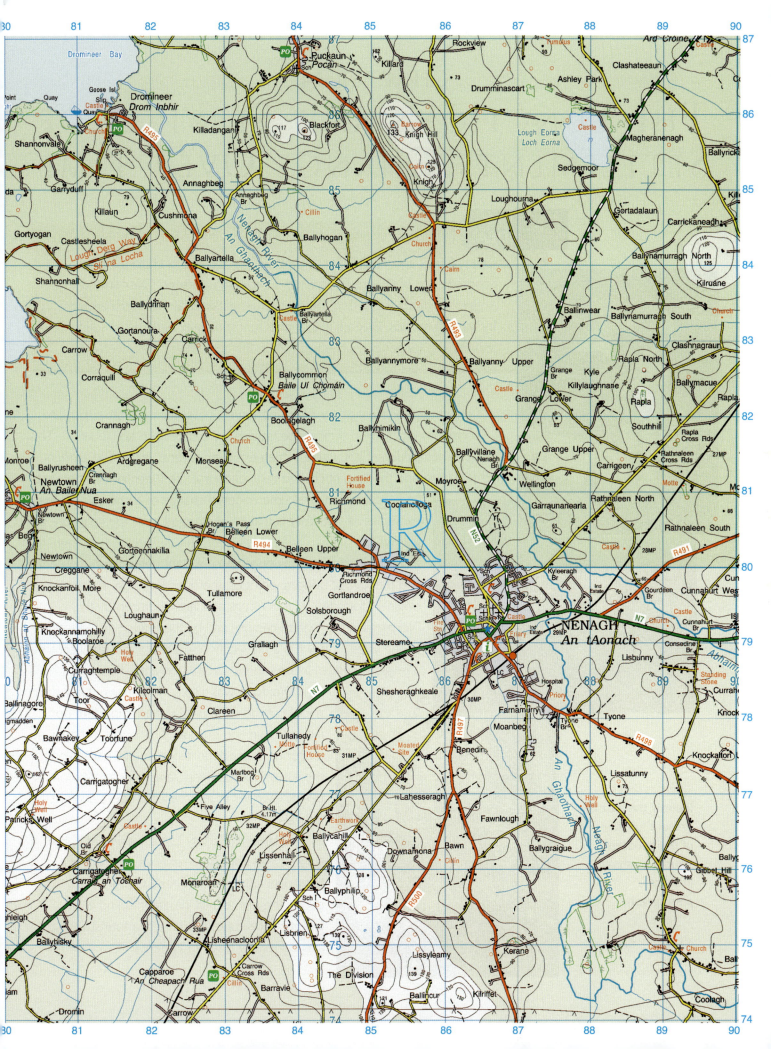

CHAPTER 14
THE FUNCTIONS AND SERVICES OF SETTLEMENTS CHANGE OVER TIME

KEY IDEA!

Cities, towns and villages are dynamic. They are and need to be in a constant state of change in order to survive and prosper. Over time the original functions that led to their initial foundation may be overshadowed by other functions. Indeed, the original functions may become obsolete and may no longer play an active role in the settlement's daily life.

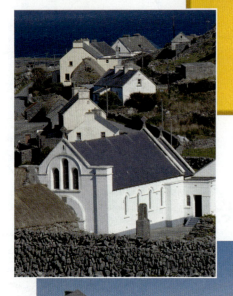

Settlements, and especially cities and towns, never remain static: they are constantly changing in their shape, size, plan, architecture and function. This becomes evident if you visit a settlement over several years. The amount of change and the kind of change vary, of course, between one settlement and another but all in time undergo change of some sort. Some examples of settlements that have changed over the years are as follows.

Limerick City was once an important defensive settlement and the lowest bridging point on the river Shannon. It was originally founded by the Vikings and later captured by the Normans in the twelfth century and by the English in 1691 after a long siege. Today it is a university city, a major industrial centre, a religious centre, a commercial centre and a market town.

Wexford was also a Viking town. Until the middle of this century it was an important port facing Britain and Europe. This port function is no longer of major importance due to silting along the estuary of the river Slaney. Today Wexford is best known for its international opera and arts festival.

Killaloe in County Clare was, as its name suggests, an important religious centre and a busy river port on the Grand Canal system during the eighteenth, nineteenth and early twentieth centuries. Today it is a tourist centre and dormitory town of Limerick.

Class activity
Identify the past or present functions of the buildings/structures shown in these photographs.

THE FUNCTIONS AND SERVICES OF SETTLEMENTS CHANGE OVER TIME

Cities acquire a distinctiveness that comes largely from their physical characteristics: the layout of streets, the presence of monuments, buildings and their architecture. All these factors reflect a city's history, its physical environment and its people's social and cultural values. Like textbooks, they can be read and analysed to see how, when and why they have developed.

Examine the nearest town to your school. Find out how the functions of this town have changed over the past century. A map of the town may help you to do this. This could form the basis of a fieldwork exercise.

Case Study: Caher in County Tipperary – a market town

Caher in County Tipperary is a busy market town

The original functions of some settlements may no longer be active. However, many towns still offer some old functions, such as market function or port function.

Caher originally had a defence function. The word 'Caher' suggests the town began as a stone fort in Celtic times. In Norman times it developed into a large town that included such buildings as an abbey, a mill and a castle. The castle was built on an island in the River Suir. Later and over time, other functions were added that increased the prosperity of the town and helped it survive and develop into the busy town that it is today.

As settlements grow over time they add new functions and lose some of their older functions/services.

THE DYNAMICS OF SETTLEMENT

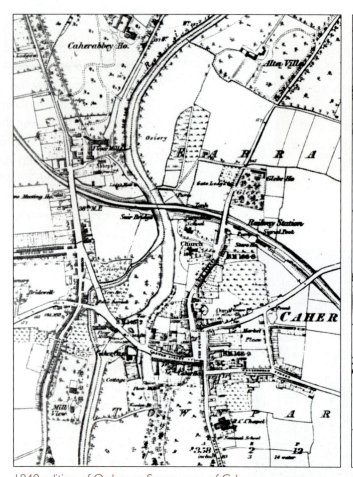

1840 edition of Ordnance Survey map of Caher

1905 edition of Ordnance Survey map of Caher

2003 edition of Ordnance Survey map of Caher town (Scale 1:50,000)

Class activity
1. Carefully examine the maps on this page and the photograph on the next page. Then identify how the services and functions of Caher have changed over time.
2. Identify one area of old industrial buildings. Then:
(a) describe the buildings; (b) explain why this site was chosen for industry in the past; (c) explain why this building style is no longer used for industry; (d) explain why this industrial site is no longer desirable for modern industry; (e) explain the advantages of the modern industrial site in the right foreground when compared to this older site described in (d) above.
3. Use the photograph to draw a sketch map of Caher. On it, mark and name: (a) the main streets and river; (b) six areas of different land use/function.

Change over time could form the basis of a good field study: old town/new town.

THE FUNCTIONS AND SERVICES OF SETTLEMENTS CHANGE OVER TIME

THE DYNAMICS OF SETTLEMENT

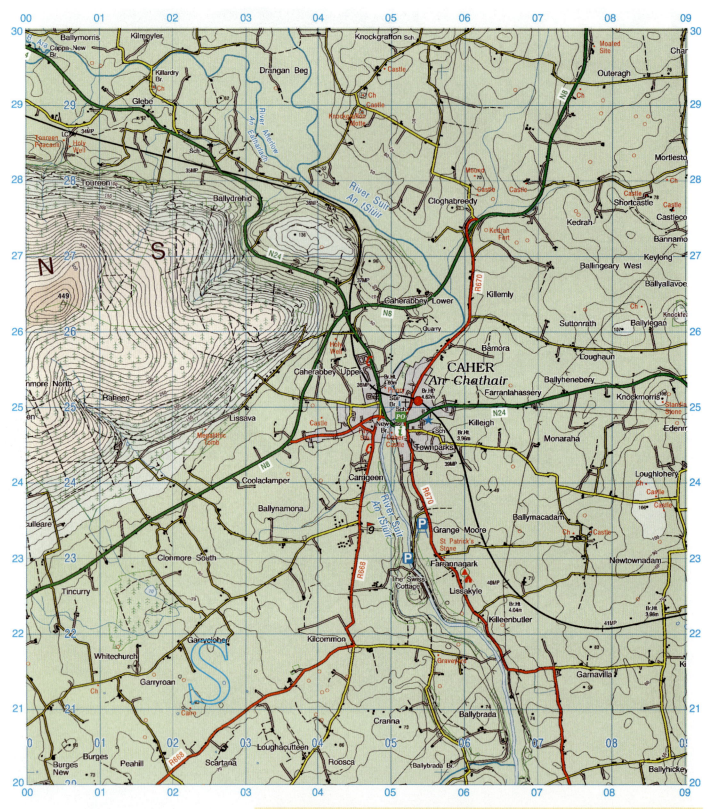

Class activity

Carefully study the Ordnance Survey map of Caher.
1. Describe the location (site and situation) of Caher.
2. From the evidence on this map only, suggest how the functions of Caher have changed over time.
3. Using the concept of Central Place Theory, explain why Caher has developed into a substantial nodal urban centre.

SECTION 5 (CHAPTERS 15–17)
URBAN LAND USE AND EXPANSION

KEY IDEA! Cities display an ever-changing land use pattern and pose planning problems.

This section examines changes in industrial, residential and commercial land uses in cities. It also examines how land values vary within cities and how these values affect where people of different incomes and cultural or racial backgrounds choose to live. As land uses change, cities expand out into the countryside, absorbing more and more farmland and natural environments.

- Chapter 15 Changing Urban Land Use Patterns
- Chapter 16 The Expansion of Cities and Pressure on Rural Land Use
- Chapter 17 Residential Areas and Segregation Within Cities

People with a common cultural background and income tend to cluster in similar areas of cities

Park West in Dublin is a new industrial and business park on the fringe of Dublin's urban region

Suburban sprawl is a major problem for twenty-first-century planners

CHAPTER 15
CHANGING URBAN LAND USE PATTERNS

LAND USE ZONES IN A MODERN IRISH CITY

The creation of different land use zones is essential in the planning and development of modern cities. These divisions are created as part of an overall plan for the renewal, revitalisation and expansion of existing major towns and cities. These plans include road and light rail developments, and new and old shopping, residential and industrial zones.

Case Study: land use zones in Galway City

Land use map of Galway City

Class activity
Carefully study the land use map of Galway City.
1. Identify the land use of the area coloured dark blue.
2. Identify some city-centre activities in this zone.
3. Which land uses in particular will preserve the city centre as the dominant commercial area of the city?

Zoning objective

- To protect residential amenities and to provide for limited associated uses
- To protect residential amenities and to provide for low density residential development
- To provide for institutional and community facility use
- To provide for city centre actives and particularly those which preserve the city centre as the dominant commercial area of the city
- To provide for light industry and commercial uses other than those reserved in CC Zone
- To provide for industrial and related uses
- To provide for recreational and amenity uses
- To provide for the development of agriculture and protect areas of visual importance and/or areas of high amenity
- To provide for the development of agriculture and to protect rural character

LAND USE ZONES AND LAND VALUES IN MODERN CITIES OF THE DEVELOPED WORLD

Over time cities have grown in size and population. Their edges are extending out into rural areas far from their oldest parts where they originally began. During their existence the patterns in land use of these settlements have changed over time. These patterns, which may show differences and similarities in land use or social groupings (high and low income areas) within a city, reflect how various cities have grown economically and socially (culturally) in response to changing conditions over many centuries. Both geographers and sociologists have proposed models in an attempt to explain how this has happened.

Regardless of size a number of different land uses or functional zones can be distinguished in most cities and towns.

To understand present and past urban land uses it is best to have a quick look at theories of urban land use development devised by three geographers who tried to explain how cities developed over time in America.

The **concentric zone theory** divides the city into circular bands. The oldest part is at the centre, which is now the central business district or CBD, with shops, offices and hotels. Some old industrial buildings may still exist but their uses may have changed as part of urban renewal schemes. It is mostly non-residential. The next band, zone 2, is where the oldest housing is located. This includes ghetto communities of poorer social groups and first-generation immigrants. Some light industry is also located there. In Ireland, some high-income residents own Georgian-style homes in well-off sections of these inner-city areas. As distance increases from the centre buildings get younger. Zone 4 includes suburban housing and older industrial estates. Zone 5 is the suburban fringe with dormitory towns.

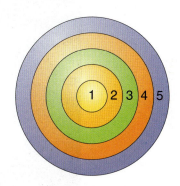

Fig. 15.1 The concentric zone theory

The **multiple nuclei theory** includes the key ideas of the concentric zone theory. However, its difference is that in some cities expansion developed around growth centres, such as hospitals, universities, shopping centres and industrial estates. This applies to many parts of Irish towns and cities outside CBD areas.

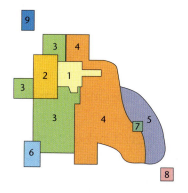

Fig. 15.2 The multiple nuclei theory

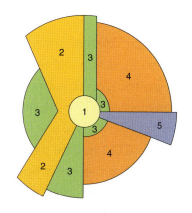

Fig. 15.3 The sector theory

1 central business district (CBD)
2 wholesale light manufacturing (transitional)
3 low-class residential
4 medium-class residential
5 high-class residential
6 heavy manufacturing
7 outlying business district
8 residential suburb
9 industrial suburb

> **Remember**
> Use these theories only as a basis for understanding change in land use over time.

The **sector theory** suggests that land uses near the central business district grew outwards as sectors or wedges along main routes. As land uses attract similar land uses, it concentrates a function in a particular area and that land use will form a wedge shape over time as the city expands. This suggests, for example, that if an area in the nineteenth century was one of low-income housing, then a wedge of low-income housing would develop at that side of the city over time. If another area had light industry then a wedge of industry would develop.

Most cities, however, display some aspects of each theory.

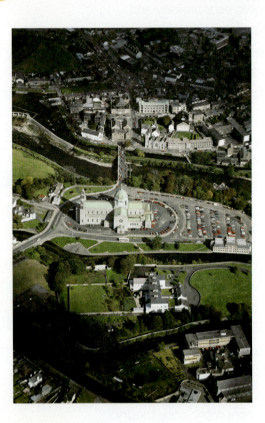

Identify the various land uses visible on this photograph of Galway City

Central Business District (CBD)

The CBD is the heart of the city. It is a city's main commercial, financial, administrative and transport centre. Some of its characteristics are as follows.
- It contains the major department stores and specialist shops.
- It has the highest land values in the city.
- It is constantly undergoing structural change to keep shops and offices at the highest modern standards.
- It contains the tallest buildings in the city.
- It has the greatest concentration of pedestrians and shoppers, e.g. Grafton Street in Dublin.

> **Class activity**
> 1. Which is the oldest part of most cities?
> 2. Which is the youngest part?
> 3. Why do most people prefer to do their Christmas shopping in the CBD?
> 4. What other shopping areas are attractive for shopping?

The competition for space and consequently **high land values** result in the very **intensive use of land within the CBD**. This is achieved by the construction of multi-storey buildings to increase floor space. Some cities limit the height of buildings. Others, such as New York, have very high buildings. In such places, the elevator or lift forms a vital link in the transport system.

On examination of the different urban functions (which include retailing, wholesaling, office accommodation and residential space) it is apparent that they vary in their ability to bid or pay for accessible locations. Also, the need for a high degree of access varies between functions. This results in the value of land declining from the centre to the edge of town.

Because the present CBD may be the original core of a city it included in the past a mixture of land uses, including residential housing, warehouses, small factories and shops. But gradually increasing land values and changing technology have pushed many of these original land uses/activities out to suburban areas. In recent decades in Ireland planning authorities have sought an orderly distribution of these land uses by creating separate zones for individual land uses, such as industrial, residential and commercial activities.

CHANGING URBAN LAND USE PATTERNS

Industrial Zones

There has been considerable movement in the location of industry in urban areas over time. Industry in the early ninteenth century was located in what are now parts of the inner city. These areas could provide a large workforce to sustain the mills, steelworks and heavy engineering on land that had not yet been built on. These industrial areas were located alongside rivers, canals and later railways, for transporting raw materials and finished products. Some industries, such as printers and bakeries, still retain their inner-city sites.

Since the 1950s many of these inner-city zones have suffered from industrial decline due to the closure of some factories and the movement of others to edge-of-city sites, such as Long-Mile Road and Park West in Dublin. Entire communities in many industrial cities of the English Midlands were supported by coal-mining, and when these collieries closed it became essential in inner-city areas to replace coal-mining activities with Enterprise Zones (EZs), where new small industries could operate successfully.

Manufacturing industry that relies on **bulk transport**, such as large ships, for the movement of bulky raw materials or finished products is attracted to **port areas within coastal cities** and towns. Deep water facilities, such as those at Foynes on the Shannon estuary, Dublin port and docks, Waterford on the River Suir and Ringaskiddy's deep water facilities in Cork Harbour encourage industry to cluster around these areas. Such industries include chemicals, oil refining, heavy metal and engineering, power stations and fish processing.

Business Parks

Most **modern industry** is 'light', footloose and clean when compared to older heavy industry. Such modern industry is located in industrial estates near to present city boundaries. Warehousing estates, business and science parks are generally located on large areas of cheap land with new buildings and modern technology, and with access to ring roads and motorways.

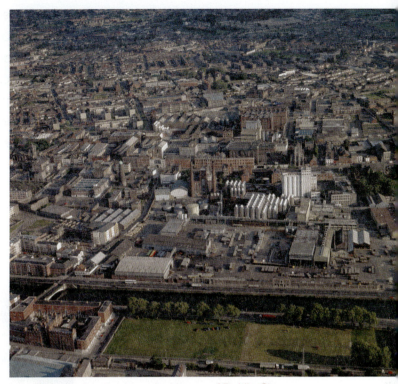

Identify the various land uses in this part of Dublin City

Identify the dominant land use in this photo

URBAN LAND USE AND EXPANSION

Case Study: Tokyo city

Tokyo developed around the castle of Edo Shogunate, near the present Imperial Palace. Later, religious, cultural and financial districts developed to the north and east. Over many centuries the mainly wooden-built city was destroyed many times by earthquakes and bombing. Because of this, old land use zones were lost when the city was rebuilt. The modern city has no single CBD. Instead it has many individual centres, each with its own specialised land use, such as government offices, finance, shopping, entertainment, transport and education. Most of these land use areas are linked by a network of railways that form a circle within the city.

Tokyo city

Out-of-town shopping centres often form the hub of new edge cities

The desire for accessibility to customers affects the spacing and siting of shopping centres and shops. The spacing of these centres corresponds to the influence of Central Place Theory, range and threshold (see page 95). In **small towns**, the **central area** is the only shopping district. Next are the **regional shopping centres that serve large parts of the suburbs and their hinterlands**. Some cater for low-income groups, while other centres cater for middle- and higher-income shoppers.

RETAIL LAND USE

Edge Cities or Suburban Downtowns

Great changes have occurred in the shopping behaviour of customers and the location and character of the shopping environment. In Britain, the USA and other industrialised countries of the developed world, new edge cities are developing as a consequence of out-of-town shopping centres. These shopping centres are developing on **cheaper land beyond the edge of existing cities.** There are two types: those that include food outlets, and those that comprise only non-food outlets. **Their aim is to capture wealthy mobile customers**, and sites near major motorway exchanges (meeting places of motorways) are chosen for their development. Some of these out-of-town developments have **attracted offices, hotels, numerous department stores, industrial parks, entertainment facilities such as sports stadia, and vast parking for up to 90,000 cars** with additional space for hundreds of buses. Some are becoming so large that they are termed **suburban downtowns** or **edge cities**. One example is Tyson's Corner in Virginia, USA.

As these suburban downtowns flourish, they attract tens of thousands of local residents who organise their lives around them. They offer workplaces, shopping, leisure activities and all other elements of a complete urban environment. The traditional **CBD is becoming less important** for goods and services. It increasingly serves the less affluent residents of inner city areas and those working downtown in offices and factories. The rise of these outer cities/suburban downtowns/edge cities has produced a new multi-centred urban land use zoning pattern. This consists of the traditional CBD, as well as a set of increasingly equally important suburban downtowns, with each servicing a different and self-sufficient surrounding hinterland.

The creation of a multi-centred urban model reduces potential traffic from the central city area. It also creates separate, distinct, economic, social and politically independent urban districts.

> In Britain in 2000, up to 40 per cent of retail sales were from out-of-town locations, compared with 5 per cent in 1980. In some areas planners are considering a change of attitude for new developments that are likely to make a serious impact on the vitality of the CBDs of the nearby cities/towns.

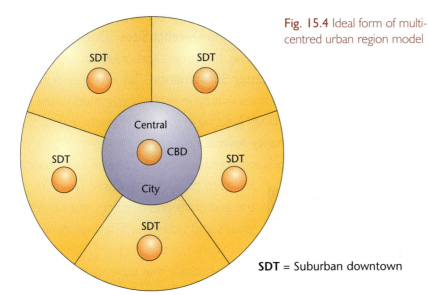

Fig. 15.4 Ideal form of multi-centred urban region model

SDT = Suburban downtown

> Suburban shopping centres in Ireland offer many attractions for shoppers. List the advantages of suburban shopping centres. List the disadvantages of shopping in CBD areas.

LAND USE ZONES IN MODERN CITIES OF THE DEVELOPING WORLD

Although the development of cities in developing countries has varied origins there are many common threads that have prompted geographers to create models of land use. One of these models is 'the Latin American city'. This model may be applied to developing cities in other parts of the world and it includes both sectors and concentric zones.

- **The CBD.** This is the primary business, employment and entertainment focus of the entire city. It includes modern high-rise buildings and old colonial buildings. When the Spanish colonisers laid out their New World cities they created a **central square**, or **plaza**, dominated by a church and surrounded by **imposing government buildings**, such as Plaza Bolívar in cities in Colombia. Early in the

Class activity
1. What are edge cities or suburban downtowns?
2. In which type of country are these located?
3. Are there any suburban downtowns in Ireland? Explain.

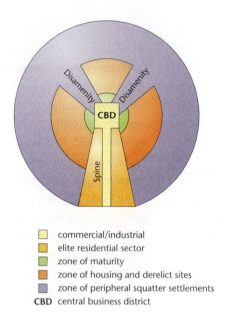

- commercial/industrial
- elite residential sector
- zone of maturity
- zone of housing and derelict sites
- zone of peripheral squatter settlements
- CBD central business district

Fig. 15.5 A generalised model of Latin American city structure

development of South American cities, the plaza formed the **hub and focus of the city**, surrounded by shopping streets and arcades. Eventually the city outgrew its old centre and new commercial districts formed elsewhere within the CBD. This left the plaza to serve as a link with the colonial past.

- **The Spine.** Radiating outward from the core along the most important routeway is a **commercial zone surrounded by an elite residential sector**. This widening corridor is essentially an extension of the CBD, with offices, shops, high-quality housing for the high-income groups (upper and upper-middle class), restaurants, theatres, golf courses and parks.
- **Zone of Maturity.** This zone in the inner city contains the **best housing** outside the spine sector, attracting middle-income/middle-class people who invest their money in renovating old 'good' houses.
- **Zone of Housing and Derelict Sites.** This is a zone of **modest housing** giving way to derelict and unkempt areas.
- **Zone of Squatter Settlements.** This is home to **impoverished** and **unskilled** hordes that have recently migrated to the city from rural areas. Although housing in this ring consists mainly of teeming, **high-density shanty towns**, residents here are surprisingly optimistic about finding work and eventually bettering their living conditions. This is achieved through unlicensed selling of goods, such as arts and crafts and clothing, and services, such as car repairs and odd jobs. Their willingness to engage in hard work has transformed many shanty towns into hives of activity that raise many residents towards a middle-income/middle-class existence.

Many shanty dwellers are able to improve their neighbourhoods through self-help projects

Class activity
1. Describe the characteristics of CBD areas in South American cities and explain their origin.
2. What characteristics, if any, does Dublin's CBD share with these cities?
3. Which land use zone is common to all cities Developing Countries due to migration effects?

CHAPTER 16
THE EXPANSION OF CITIES AND PRESSURE ON RURAL LAND USE

KEY IDEA! As cities expand, green belts within cities or rural environments on the edge of cities come under increasing pressure to change their use.

Urban expansion is a world-wide problem. There has been rapid growth both in the number of cities and the expansion of urban areas out into the countryside. This is especially true in developing countries where some city boundaries, such as Sao Paulo in Brazil, extend as far as 100 kilometres from the CBD. Some regions, such as the United States, display such urban expansion that the term **megalopolis** has been applied to the clustering of its cities to form vast urban environments. Two city clusters, one along the north-eastern seaboard from Boston to Washington DC, which includes New York, Philadelphia and Baltimore and the second, Los Angeles, which includes Long Beach, Hollywood, Anaheim, Pasadena, Burbank and Century City, each forms a 'megalopolis'.

Today, with 71 per cent of its population living in towns and cities, Europe ranks among the world's most highly urbanised areas. This is especially true in northern and western Europe where 84 and 79 per cent of the population respectively live in urban areas. This percentage rises even higher in certain places: in Belgium, 97 per cent; in the United Kingdom, 90 per cent; and in both Germany and Denmark, 85 per cent. In the Netherlands the expansion of the **Randstad** region was happening so fast that government controls were introduced to preserve the greenheart within its horseshoe-shaped conurbation. These controls included both the creation of growth centres to limit future expansion to just a few centres and the creation of overspill towns, such as Almere, on newly reclaimed polderlands.

Parks, no matter how small, such as this one in the centre background, offer recreational areas within cities

Green Belts and Natural Areas within Cities

Green belts are open spaces of agricultural land, parks or areas of woodland within large towns and cities. They are specifically designed to break up the monotony of urban development such as housing estates and industrial zones. They are designed by urban planners and become permanent features when legislated by local government.

URBAN LAND USE AND EXPANSION

Green belts in urban areas have many purposes:
1. They prevent continuous development in large towns and cities, which improves the quality of urban environments.
2. They provide sports fields, areas for leisure walks and runs, golf courses and so on.
3. Urban recreation areas such as Central Park in New York City, St Stephen's Green and Phoenix Park in Dublin, and Eyre Square in Galway provide a welcome relief from an office environment at lunch hour and a pleasant place for local residents.

Parks such as St Stephen's Green provide urban dwellers with areas that allow quality time away from the bustle of busy city living

As cities and conurbations grow, more and more pressure is put on existing green belts and farmland for urban expansion. Dublin's planned expansion over the past 30 years has been greatly influenced by the re-zoning of many of its green belt areas. These changes were introduced by local government councillors against the wishes of the city planners who initially devised them. Today's green belts and farmland continue to struggle for survival due to the increased demand for housing by our growing young adult population.

Large cities such as London continue to expand at the expense of the countryside. There are plans for 20 new towns for the greater London area. This proposal is facing opposition from environmentalists, who argue that such development will counteract urban renewal schemes within the city and have a severe impact on existing green belt areas.

SUSTAINABLE DEVELOPMENT OF GREEN BELTS

Urban development should include the maintenance of natural areas and the protection of their wildlife populations so that people can have contact with nature close to their homes.

There are also political factors that must be addressed. Management of natural and national parks is increasingly being separated from local and regional authorities, such as county councils and city corporations, even though cities and parks depend on each other. Because the people who use natural parks have a wide range of interests that regularly conflict with each other, the relevant agencies and the communities involved must be brought together to develop strategies so that nature reserves can be managed successfully. Experience also shows that vandalism and damage are greatly reduced where there is a sense of involvement in a local project and when local people feel they

THE EXPANSION OF CITIES AND PRESSURE ON RURAL LAND USE

Water as a resource has many people-friendly uses in an urban environment

Green belts may be used for many recreational activities such as cycling, jogging or walking

have a stake in an urban green space. Such issues might include re-zoning, access and visitor pressure in regions of high population densities. Management must combine ecological awareness with understanding of the needs of the urban population.

Future success in this area requires the marriage of natural areas around towns and cities with green areas within cities. For example, for a city child, a widening experience might include contact with nature in a pond or natural area within walking distance of his or her home or school, extending to a natural area in a local river valley or town park, then moving to a nature reserve within the city and finally going out to the national park on the fringe of the city.

> Children who have been exposed to natural areas are more inclined to be better aware of the advantages of keeping close to nature and being responsible citizens.

Class activity
1. Carefully study the photographs above. Then explain the advantages of green spaces, such as those in the photographs, in urban areas. In your answer refer to two aspects and in each case give a well-developed explanation.
2. Identify two types of land use development that cause Irish cities to expand into the countryside.
3. Explain how these types of developments impact on traffic flow across and to Ireland's largest cities.
4. Explain how the expansion of Dublin has affected (a) local green belt regions; (b) quality of life of Dublin's citizens; (c) quality of life of commuters to Dublin.

Chapter 17
Residential Areas and Segregation Within Cities

KEY IDEA! People with different incomes, cultural or racial backgrounds tend to cluster in separate parts of a city.

Does this dwelling belong to a low-, middle- or high-income couple?

Residential land use occupies between 72 and 80 per cent of most cities and towns. The characteristics of citizens and the areas where they live vary greatly between different parts of the city. Dwellings differ according to their age, arrangement, style, building material, condition and size. However, they may be classed into two groups: single family homes; and multi-family homes.

Single family homes range from scraps of metal and wood in shanty towns to small nineteenth-century terraced red-brick houses in inner city areas to luxury villas set in large gardens in wealthy residential districts.

Multi-family homes include three- or four-storey tenements housing two or three families and modern high-rise apartment blocks accommodating hundreds of families. These are most often found in inner city areas. The principal factors for choosing a home include type of house, price, location and neighbourhood environment.

Income is the most important influence on choice of home. For instance, parents may have a large family, but if they are poor they cannot afford a large detached home in a wealthy neighbourhood. Poor parents are generally confined to choosing smaller houses in corporation housing estates or larger ones in poor condition. For people who **do not have cars** and for whom **transport costs would erode** a large part of their income, **access to public transport**, bus or rail, and being close to their place of work are important.

Many old neighbourhoods have been refurbished and are thriving residential areas once again

Some housing estates built in the 1970s are poorly maintained. Burnt-out cars are a common sight in some of these low-income estates.

RESIDENTIAL SEGREGATION

The factors that influence the choice and purchase of individual homes lead to the segregation of people into **separate areas** of a city. A particular location and environment in a city will attract a certain type of dwelling and a certain income group. For example, local authorities provide subsidised housing for the poorer sector of the population. Some developments may be for those with large families and others for older citizens. Such local government developments may contribute to segregation because of the high density of homes in some estates such as South Hill and Moyross in Limerick and Ballymun in Dublin.

Other multi-storey corporation flats in Dublin's inner city have created zones of low-income residents, many of whom are long-term unemployed people. These neighbourhoods contrast greatly with wealthier areas of Dublin, such as around Ballsbridge and Donnybrook in Dublin 4.

> Identify different areas in your nearest city where people with high, middle and low incomes reside.

Dublin Corporation has housed many low-income families in inner-city apartment blocks

High-quality, high-cost housing forms distinct zones in parts of Dublin's urban area

Some residential groups interact with developers and planners to produce areas with compatible neighbours with whom they have most in common. They may act to exclude some people and land uses from their neighbourhoods in order to preserve the 'atmosphere' of their area and the value of their property. This discrimination has been highlighted in some Irish cities and towns in relation to the settling in housing estates of some people from the travelling community.

Ghettos

A ghetto is a section of a city settled by a minority racial, religious or national group in which the majority of the inhabitants have particular socio-economic characteristics that distinguish them from the urban population as a whole. The term ghetto originally referred to sections of European cities where Jews settled or were forced to live. Today, the term is applied to slum areas where black

A ghetto community offers support and security for members of minority ethnic or economic groups

people and other minority groups, such as Puerto Ricans in New York, Chinese in San Francisco, Roman Catholics in Belfast, North Africans in Paris and lower castes in Calcutta, have particular characteristics in common.

The ghetto is usually a product of discrimination by society against the group concerned, but it can also be created by forces of security or bonding within the group. An under-privileged group that has limited access to jobs and houses is often forced by circumstances to live in the poorest part of the city near to the centre or CBD. Unity within a group is reflected in the desire of many minority groups to maintain their identity as a people with a separate history and culture, and this can be more readily achieved by living together in one area. The ghetto offers common interests and friendships, even if living conditions are poor.

Uniting forces are particularly strong amongst recent immigrant groups who may cluster together for support in a new society. There may be relations or neighbours from home already living in the ghetto, making accommodation easier to find, and cultural identity is maintained. Irish emigrants over the past two centuries lived in areas of cities where large numbers of Irish people were already living. Such areas include Camden Town in London and the Bronx in New York.

Cities that experience high rates of in-migration, such as American cities, have tended to become structured into a series of concentric zones of neighbourhoods of different ethnic groups, income levels and social status through processes of **invasion and succession** and **congregation**. **Invasion and succession** is a process of **neighbourhood change** whereby **one social or ethnic group succeeds another** by increasing their numbers and becoming the dominant group.

Congregation is the **clustering of neighbourhoods** of specific groups of people, which over time develop into one large community with certain criteria in common. This occurs when similar kinds of households go through similar search patterns, make similar decisions about where to live and eventually settle in areas where there are people with whom they can readily identify.

Social segregation is clearly visible today in many American cities. New York, for example, has many areas where ethnic groups form clearly defined residential zones. These include Harlem for black people, Chinatown for Chinese and Little Italy for Italians.

> Individuals from many European countries lived within 'ethnic areas' by choice rather than by force. As they prospered, they became more secure and moved to middle-class American suburbs.

Class activity
1. Explain the advantages of local authority housing to some urban dwellers.
2. What is a ghetto? Explain.
3. Explain the terms (a) invasion and succession; (b) congestion. Explain why these can be positive forces within residential areas.

Shanty Towns

Shanty town development is associated with cities of the developing world. They are slum areas characterised by shacks set on unpaved streets, often with open sewers and no basic services. (See page 146.)

Shanty town dwellings are built from galvanise, timber sheets, plastic and any other materials available

Section 6 (Chapters 18–24)
Urban Problems and Planning Strategies

 **Problems can develop from the growth of towns and cities.**

This section examines some problems that can develop from the growth of cities in developed and developing countries that lead to a deterioration in the living environment. It also looks at some ways that urban authorities have attempted to reduce these difficulties by developing strategies for future sustainable development.

- Chapter 18   Urban Problems in the Developed World
- Chapter 19   Urban Decay, Urban Sprawl and the Absence of Community
- Chapter 20   Conservation of the Built Environment
- Chapter 21   Urban Growth and the Environment
- Chapter 22   Urban Planning and Urban Renewal in Irish Cities
- Chapter 23   Expansion and Problems in Developing World Cities
- Chapter 24   The Future of Urbanism

Dublin's new metro system will help reduce traffic within its CBD

New methods of dealing with increasing levels of urban waste need to be put into practise

Acceptable housing standards are sadly lacking in many cities of the developing world

CHAPTER 18
URBAN PROBLEMS IN THE DEVELOPED WORLD

KEY IDEA! Historical development and traffic patterns influence traffic flow within cities.

TRAFFIC MOVEMENT AND CONGESTION IN TOWNS AND CITIES

Traffic movement and congestion in towns and cities are two of the most consistent and pressing problems in urban areas of the developed world. Roads provide the most flexible and cost-effective means of transport because they enable a door-to-door transfer of people and goods at reasonable cost. However, because of its efficiency, road transport has become the most desirable and also most over-used form of travel within towns and cities.

Vehicles use roads for a number of purposes, such as:
- The transfer of people to and from work, shopping and leisure.
- The transfer of raw materials and manufactured products.

Roads and streets are the veins and arteries of urban centres and are vital to the life of a city. They also influence the land use zoning of urban areas and directly affect the shape and direction of urban expansion. In many instances they add to an individual city or town's character, as in the case of San Francisco's steep streets and its trams on Powell's Street or the unplanned nature of the streets in Kinsale, County Cork.

The absence of vehicles from some city centre areas has also added renewed character to urban areas. Three main factors influence traffic movement and congestion in cities and towns.
- Street patterns.
- Patterns of traffic movement.
- Traffic control.

Unplanned streets in old cities create congestion and poor traffic flow. What evidence in this photograph of Kinsale in County Cork indicates that part of the town is unplanned and could cause traffic congestion?

How Street Patterns Affect Movement and Congestion

Unplanned streets

With the exception of new towns, most urban areas developed over a long period of time.

- Most of our coastal cities were founded by the Vikings, and most of Ireland's other cities and towns began either in Norman or Plantation times. The oldest parts of these settlements are located in their Central Business Districts (CBDs) and some streets are narrow and unplanned. Their individual layout was influenced by factors such as the character of the site, the time of origin, the nature of urban development and the form of land ownership. Street patterns may vary from one part of a town to another, indicating development over a long time.

- Unplanned streets developed in piecemeal fashion during medieval times. Many of them are winding and narrow, some only a few metres wide in places. On-street parking on such streets creates obstacles to the free movement of traffic. Sidewalks may even be too narrow for pedestrians, who may be forced to walk on the street itself. Such is the case in Wexford town.

Many of Wexford's streets are narrow

- Many unplanned streets meet at irregular angles where markets were once held. Because medieval towns were generally small, transport was by foot or horse-drawn carts. Movement was slow but constant. Some towns, such as Kilmallock in County Limerick, still retain their **old gate arches** that controlled the entry and exit of people and goods into and out of the town. Traffic movement is easily regulated on wide planned streets where one-way traffic systems work well in association with on-street parking.

- **Off-street parking in multi-storey car parks** or in areas where buildings have been demolished reduces traffic congestion in these places. Traffic movement is generally confined to a **one-way system** in these narrow and winding streets. If on-street parking is allowed it is usually **confined to one side** of the street only. In such cases single and double yellow lines along the street edge prevent daytime parking to avoid congestion. Parking may be **allowed within white rectangular boxes**.

Medieval gate entrances are still common in old Italian towns such as Assisi

Planned street patterns

Roman towns were laid out in **rectangular blocks**, and their streets formed a **grid plan**. Many towns in Croatia, Italy, France and England are of Roman origin. The defensive town walls usually formed a square or rectangle. There were four main gates and the two connecting main streets intersected at right angles. This pattern was extensively used

URBAN PROBLEMS AND PLANNING STRATEGIES

This grid plan in Washington DC is typical of American planned cities

during **colonial times** throughout America. In some of Ireland's largest cities, such as Limerick, Dublin and Derry, buildings form rectangular blocks with parallel main streets and others intersecting at right angles. This pattern evolved mainly because land was sold in regular blocks rather than because of any formal urban planning. Traffic movement is easily regulated in these cities because streets are wide, on-street parking is allowed and one-way traffic systems work well. However, it is the **increased volume** of urban traffic since the 1950s in America, and since the 1970s in Ireland, that has caused extensive congestion within CBDs and on roads approaching urban settlements.

Patterns of traffic movement

Traffic movement in urban areas may be divided into two main categories:
- Traffic into and within the CBD and suburban downtowns.
- Traffic within and between suburbs.

> The increased volume of urban traffic in recent decades causes constant congestion within cities of the developed world.

Traffic into and within city and suburban downtown centres is usually to work or school, occurs in the morning between 7am and 9.30am and is called the morning rush hour. In the late afternoon between 3.30pm and 6.30pm the return journey from school and shopping is followed by the journey from work. This peak time is called evening rush hour. It is during these peak times that traffic congestion is at its most extreme. It is at present the greatest problem that cities have to overcome. Traffic jams many kilometres long and up to three lanes wide are a regular occurrence during the rush hour in major cities of the developed world.

The expansion of towns and cities in the developed world out into the countryside has created **urban sprawl** on a massive scale. A substantial number of car owners from these suburban areas use their vehicles during rush hours. This movement clogs main arterial roads, motorways and suburban streets. On some occasions it may be quicker to gain access to the motorway or freeway to shop in a regional suburban downtown area some distance away than to go to the nearest local shops.

Traffic within and between suburbs is of two main types:
1. Movement from home to 'suburban downtowns'.
2. Movement from home to leisure/shopping centres and schools.

Weekend and late evening patterns are different from those in the working week. Weekend movements are often from the cities to suburban shopping centres and to rural areas for leisure and sporting activities.

Class activity

1. Explain three ways that street patterns influence traffic flow in Irish towns.
2. Explain why towns of colonial origin differ in their street plan to other older towns.
3. Explain the main causes of traffic congestion in Irish towns today.

Although Dublin City has expanded its transport system to service the expanding Dublin region it has generally not kept pace with developments. This has resulted in significant traffic congestion within the city. Some recent developments, such as the opening of the **M50 motorway** and **improvements to the N7**, and the **M1 to Belfast** have improved traffic flow. The **Dart commuter railway** provides an efficient north-south service linking suburban coastal towns such as Howth and Bray to Dublin. A new rail service, the **Luas system,** and a **Port Tunnel** are part of ongoing improvements to ease traffic congestion in the Greater Dublin region.

Dual carriageways in cities such as Dublin are choked with traffic

Traffic control

Most cities, other than modern new towns, were not designed to cope with the demands of modern traffic movements. Many were initially constructed at a time when road transport was confined to movement on foot or by horse. Nevertheless, traffic must be monitored and controlled to deal with present traffic problems. There are two general approaches to reduce the problem:

1. Provide more road space and off-street parking areas to ease the problem of increasing numbers of cars. This can be achieved by urban renewal schemes. Such schemes allow planners and architects in inner city areas to:
   - Construct new multi-storey car parks.
   - Create new streets by demolishing old buildings.
   - One-way streets, restricted turns (no left or right turn) at street junctions, clearways (single and double yellow lines), parking meters, disc parking, multi-storey car parks and video camera monitoring.
   - Ring roads to keep as much traffic away from the CBD as possible. In addition, the creation of raised motorways through inner city areas is a possibility but this has been opposed in many places for environmental reasons. It has already been used in multi-centred cities, such as Los Angeles. Brussels and Stockholm also have raised motorways through their CBDs.

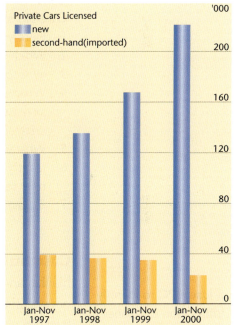

Fig. 18.1 Private car licensed figures for Ireland during the late 1990s

Class activity
Carefully examine the chart for licensed vehicles 1997–2000.
1. What trend is evident from the chart?
2. How many vehicles were licensed in 1997?
3. How many vehicles were licensed in 2000?
4. What problems has this trend created for Irish cities and towns? Explain fully.
5. Explain ways to reduce traffic congestion within urban regions.

2. Develop an efficient public transport system, either above or below ground, or both, with frequent and fast services. London, New York and Paris have these services and they are very effective. See the section on improvements to Dublin congestion on page 141.

Table 18.1 Number of mechanically propelled vehicles by taxation class 1960–2001

Year	Private cars	Goods vehicles	Agricultural tractors etc	Motor cycles	Others	Total
1960	169,681	43,530	37,719	41,467	10,370	302,767
1970	389,338	48,751	65,975	40,951	13,388	558,403
1980	734,371	65,052	69,118	28,488	14,002	911,031
1985	709,546	93,369	68,552	26,025	17,266	914,758
1990	796,408	143,166	72,814	22,744	19,127	1,054,259
1995	990,384	141,785	77,925	23,452	28,957	1,262,503
1998	1,196,901	170,866	78,047	24,398	40,641	1,510,853
1999	1,269,245	188,814	70,591	26,677	47,829	1,608,156
2001	1,384,704	219,510	73,719	32,913	58,838	1,769,684

Class activity
Carefully study the figures in Table 18.1.
1. Identify the total increase in vehicles from 1960 to 2001.
2. Which category of vehicle increased the most? Give details.
3. What percentage increase occurred in the vehicle type mentioned in question 2?
4. What effects, in your opinion, have occurred in urban areas as a consequence of the increase in this vehicle type? In your answer, refer to traffic flow, environment and urban limits.
5. What vehicle type increased the least?
6. Identify the causes and effects of the increase in the 'goods vehicle' class. In your answer, refer to employment, standard of living and urban zones.
7. Explain reasons for the trend in vehicle ownership between 1980 and 1985.

Case Study: New York

Manhattan Island forms the CBD of New York City and is the core of a vast urban region of over 250 square kilometres that contains 20 million people. It has many distinctive land use areas, including Central Park, mid-town and downtown Manhattan. Harlem is a low-income residential zone while Chinatown and Little Italy are cultural or ethnic communities that have formed around the city's core.

Because it is located on an island, entrance to Manhattan is gained by either bridges or tunnels across the Hudson and East Rivers. Morning rush hour consists of continuous traffic jams as out-of-town traffic is confined to these access points leading into Manhattan. Each day, traffic delays cost New York City's businesses about 500,000 work hours. That translates into US$4 billion yearly in lost production. Public transport helps reduce traffic overcrowding by keeping an estimated half a million cars out of Manhattan's Central Business District (CBD) each day. Without public transit, traffic in the CBD would more than double, and New York City traffic outside the CBD would increase by about 20 per cent.

Use a PC to identify other land use zones in Manhattan Island. These should include ethnic/cultural areas, high-income and low-income residential areas, industrial areas and shopping areas.

URBAN PROBLEMS IN THE DEVELOPED WORLD

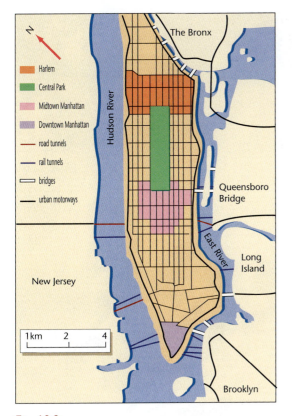

Fig. 18.2

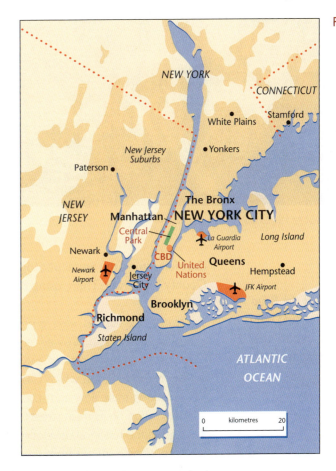

Fig. 18.3

Identify the land uses of the following areas in New York City: Wall Street, Park Avenue, Madison Avenue, Fifth Avenue and Broadway.

Class activity
Study Figs. 18.2, 18.3 and, with the aid of your atlas, do the following:
1. Identify some cities that form part of New York's Metropolitan area.
2. What advantage does the street pattern of New York have with regard to traffic flow?
3. How does the site of New York City influence traffic flow into and out of the city?
4. Explain how the public transport system within New York City reduces potential street traffic.

125

URBAN PROBLEMS AND PLANNING STRATEGIES

Cashel, County Tipperary

Class activity
Carefully study the aerial photograph of Cashel in County Tipperary. Then, using the evidence from the photo:
1. Identify the various ways in which Cashel controls its traffic flow. In your answer refer to road markings, public and private parking and urban planning.
2. Identify one way in which Cashel could radically reduce its traffic flow and so eliminate continuous congestion on its main street.
3. Explain the historical development of the town over time, using evidence from the photograph only.
4. Explain how Cashel's urban environment could be improved by its local authority, using evidence from the photograph only.

A *Rules of the Road* booklet would help you to identify the various road markings.

CHAPTER 19
URBAN DECAY, URBAN SPRAWL AND THE ABSENCE OF COMMUNITY

> **KEY IDEA!** Rapid change within cities has resulted in a number of problems for urban residents and urban planners. These problems include: zones of urban decay and urban sprawl; the absence of community.

PROBLEMS OF URBAN GROWTH

Zones of Urban Decay and Urban Sprawl

Rapid urban growth in cities has resulted in the mass movement of people from inner city communities to new homes in the suburbs. This movement has created zones of decline in some inner city areas and zones of urban sprawl at the edges of these cities.

Urban decay

Derelict buildings, poor-quality housing and the closure or movement of old industries from inner city areas has led to large-scale movement of people away from these areas. Inner city areas had many disadvantages, including:

1. Inner city areas are the oldest parts of cities. Because of this, inner cities contained a large number of old buildings and poor quality housing. The density of buildings was also high and there was little, if any, space for recreation as part of these dwellings (see Urban Renewal Programmes, page 145).

Urban decay occurs in all towns such as in this area in Armagh

2. Large numbers of young couples abandoned inner city areas for homes in the suburbs. Many of the people who remain are elderly, single, on low incomes or unemployed.

3. Some city corporations, such as Dublin Corporation, re-housed some inner city communities in the 1970s in poorly designed multi-storey buildings. Many of these high-rise buildings lacked basic facilities, such as lifts, and so presented difficulties, especially for the young and older people. In other instances entire inner city communities were re-housed in the suburbs.

URBAN PROBLEMS AND PLANNING STRATEGIES

> Bear in mind that not all inner city areas suffer high crime rates nor are they all decaying communities. Many inner city communities are thriving and take an active part in promoting innovative practices, such as adult learning and land use planning.

4. Many inner city communities have a high percentage of residents dependent on social welfare. This, in addition to high crime rates and substance abuse, creates an environment that is not attractive for investment. This in turn creates a cycle that increases social problems.
5. Constant traffic congestion, the high cost of land and ageing buildings pushed old industries from inner city areas. As modern factories prefer greenfield sites in industrial estates where all facilities are provided for industry only, most industrial parks are now located in the suburbs.

Urban sprawl

The growth of towns and cities has transformed urban living patterns. As a country develops from an agriculture-based society to an industrial economy, large-scale movement of people from rural areas to towns and cities takes place. Some 29 per cent of the world's population was living in urban areas in 1950. Today the figure is 50 per cent, and it is predicted that this figure will increase to **60 per cent by 2030**. The vast majority of these people will live either in suburbs of the developed world or in shanty towns in the developing world. As all cities increase in size, more and more agricultural land will fall victim to urban sprawl.

Car ownership. Car ownership has had a dramatic affect on the size of urban areas throughout the world. As a society gets wealthier, the greater the number of cars that are purchased. In addition, the efficiency of the motor car and the improvement in roads allows more and more people to live in suburban areas and get to work, school or to leisure facilities by car. So increased wealth has created rapid housing growth on the edges of cities and a corresponding increase in car ownership.

Access to work. The concentration of office employment and major department stores in city centre areas creates a daily routine of travel to and from work in the morning and evening. People travel from suburban housing, dormitory towns and individual homes into the city centre during rush hour. The expansion of suburbs has caused the edges of these settlements and that of the city to merge, creating a vast urban environment.

Industry. Increased traffic congestion in cities has forced all new large-scale industries to set up along the edges of cities, either in industrial parks or in land zoned for industrial development. Industries use up large amounts of land as expansion and easy access

Urban sprawl in Los Angeles has caused this urban region to spread out into the surrounding area

Many family members of working age own their own cars and commute to work daily

by large trucks to individual industries is vital to their continued success.

Absence of community

Because of overcrowding and poor-quality homes, entire inner city communities were re-housed by Dublin Corporation in suburban housing estates or multi-storey buildings (flats), such as in Ballymun in Dublin. These inner city communities were well established with many three-generation families living near each other. Once these families were moved they were separated into different suburban areas. Family support that was so important within their inner city communities was no longer present. This created insecurity and a loss of identity that could not be restored in the short term.

When young people move from inner city communities they leave behind their parents, who form a high percentage of inner city residents. When this occurs, services such as youth clubs, and community facilities such as schools, close for lack of numbers. This removes the vitality of these areas and creates a cycle of decay in inner city regions.

New urban roads help to reduce traffic congestion

Some old inner city communities have disappeared due to urban decay and migration to suburban areas

Class activity
1. Explain why some parts of Irish cities have fallen into decay over time.
2. Urban sprawl is a problem that developed during the twentieth century and is increasing at a faster rate today.
   (a) Explain three reasons for urban sprawl.
   (b) Explain two reasons for the increased rate of urban sprawl in recent decades.

Case Study: Dublin traffic

Gridlock gets Worse on Road to Success

The downside of the Celtic Tiger was highlighted in a major report on the transport sector. The report points to an explosion in the number of cars on our roads – an increase of 48 per cent since 1980.

In the first six months of 2000, there were almost 160,000 new private cars licensed, an increase of 43 per cent on the corresponding period for 1999.

'This growth has resulted in increased congestion in urban areas, as well as impacts on the environment', the report states.

'Large and small public service vehicles and school buses only constitute less than 2 per cent of the total road transport as opposed to the 79 per cent share belonging to private cars', it says.

URBAN PROBLEMS AND PLANNING STRATEGIES

Traffic jams are a regular occurrence on Dublin's M50, due to an increase in car ownership and the development of business parks in the suburbs

The main recommendation in the report for cutting overall transport problems is the curtailment of the private car with promotion of 'less damaging' modes of transport a priority.

'More environmentally friendly forms of transport should be encouraged. Walking and cycling are the least damaging methods of travel.

'However, currently just over 11 per cent of the population walk to work in the country and only 2 per cent cycle. Over half the people employed nation-wide travel to work by car, and public transport use is quite limited', the report states.

'Transport management, particularly in urban areas, requires the use of taxes and charges, to promote a shift from the car to more environmentally friendly forms of transport.

'Taxes can influence consumer choice and behaviour in favour of the more efficient and environmentally friendly transport options such as bus or train', it adds.

It also points to the need to have more buses on the roads and suggests that Quality Bus Corridors (QBCs) should be more widely introduced.

Spending more time in our cars as a result of gridlock is another by-product of our car explosion. Travel times for commuters have increased for all parts of Dublin between 1991 and 1999.

It points to a survey carried out in 1998 which showed that of 152,000 car journeys made on the M50 motorway each day, 80 per cent of vehicles carried just one person.

Action is urgently needed on the proposed fast rail link to Dublin Airport, which has an indicative timetable for completion by 2010, he said. 'This date must be significantly brought forward', he said.

Dublin's traffic congestion is now believed to be costing the economy more than £500 million a year, and the overall cost of traffic associated problems to the Republic is thought to be around £2.2 billion.

Extract taken from the *Irish Times*

Why not use your PC to check on traffic in New York and Paris?

Class activity

Carefully study the extract on pages 129–30 and Table 18.1, page 124. Then use the evidence from these sources to answer the following questions:

1. According to the article, what is the greatest cause of traffic congestion in Irish towns and cities?
2. What other factors contribute to traffic congestion in Ireland?
3. What methods, according to the article, can be introduced to reduce urban traffic?
4. What difficulties are created by traffic congestion for commuters in Dublin?

URBAN DECAY, URBAN SPRAWL AND THE ABSENCE OF COMMUNITY

Inner city areas, such as Baggot Street in Dublin, suffer from traffic congestion

O'Connell Street in Dublin has a constant heavy traffic flow

Class activity

Identify the various problems that arise as a consequence of traffic congestion in Dublin. In your answer make reference to (a) the cost of congestion to transport providers such as truck companies; (b) the environment; (c) the quality of life for commuters.

Case Study: Paris

Paris, often described as the nicest city in the world, is a large sprawling primate city that has over 10 million people. Lying at the heart of the Paris Basin, Paris is France's core area. No other city in France comes close to Paris in terms of population or centrality.

Transport. Paris has an efficient underground rail service, the Metro, that has recently been extended. It has recently built an additional 900 kilometres of motorway to cope with the projected growth of the city. The Arc de Triomphe is the centre of the city's main avenues. They radiate from a circular street that surrounds the monument. Consequently, this 'roundabout', with its twelve radiating avenues, is choked with traffic, especially at rush hour. Because Paris was a planned city its streets are wide and capable of carrying large numbers of cars.

Some historic buildings in Paris include:
- Arc de Triomphe
- Louvre
- Eiffel Tower
- Cathedral of Sacré-Coeur

Urban decay and redevelopment. Paris has many ageing industrial areas within the city where poor overcrowded communities live. It has many ghettos where Muslim immigrants and people of various nationalities from former colonies in Africa and south-east Asia reside. Urban planners have tried to solve some of these inner city problems in the following ways:
- Renewal of inner city residential areas. Over the past 20 years some 200,000 units of social housing have been built. However, affordable housing remains a problem for many Parisians and migrant workers.

URBAN PROBLEMS AND PLANNING STRATEGIES

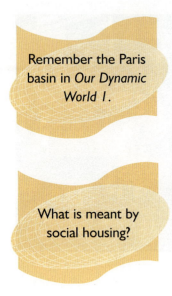

Remember the Paris basin in *Our Dynamic World 1*.

What is meant by social housing?

- A new financial centre, La Défense, was an effort to revitalise the inner city. In 1960, La Défense was an underdeveloped site not far from the city centre. By the mid-1980s it housed over 200,000 residents and 100,000 workers in newly built high-rise offices. Since 1990, over 77,000 jobs have been created in other developments around La Défense. This development has been one of the most successful schemes of urban renewal in the world.
- Eight new suburban downtowns were developed around the city to create new housing and employment, and to reduce commuter traffic to the city centre.
- Five new towns were developed outside the city. These are now well-established settlements with more than 100,000 inhabitants each.
- Eight growth centres were selected to reduce the dominance of Paris as a primate city. Roads and rail links were improved and new industries were attracted to each of these centres.

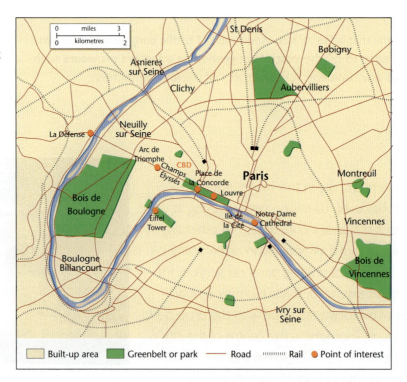

Fig. 19.1 *Use this map to identify two advantages of Paris's public transport network*

Class activity
1. Identify one region of Paris that suffers from traffic congestion.
2. Explain why congestion occurs in this area.
3. What is a ghetto? Explain.
4. Explain why Paris has large populations of many ethnic groups.
5. Explain how French planners have attempted to solve urban decay within the Paris region.
6. What is a suburban downtown? Explain fully.

CHAPTER 20
CONSERVATION OF THE BUILT ENVIRONMENT

 **KEY IDEA!** Areas and buildings of historic importance should be preserved in Irish towns and cities.

As with the natural environment, there is now much greater awareness of the value of conserving our built environment. The repair and retention of older buildings including their important architectural details, revitalises cities and towns and adds to their aesthetic value and identity. New measures to protect our heritage include:

- An obligation on local authorities to maintain a record of protected buildings as part of their development plans.
- Ensuring that, where a building is protected, the whole of the building, including interior and courtyard, is protected.
- An active role for local authorities in ensuring that protected buildings are not endangered by neglect.
- Special streetscapes and other features of interest, such as ornamental doorways and signs, need to be protected.
- Designers will have some freedom to adopt more sympathetic and appropriate approaches to the adaptation of architecturally valuable buildings for new uses. In addition, the Programme for Local Urban and Rural Development provides financial support of up to 50 per cent to local authorities and conservation groups to promote conservation measures in towns and cities.
- In cases where historic buildings or sites cannot be protected for some reason, these areas should be excavated and recorded.

As part of Limerick's Strategic Plan, specific buildings were listed for conservation. These include King John's Castle, St Mary's Cathedral and Villiers Almshouses.

> Identify some historic buildings or streets with particular charm in your town that should be preserved as part of our heritage. List the historic characteristics of each of your choices.

Class activity
1. List the characteristics of each of the buildings in the photographs that identify them as suitable for preservation.
2. What advantages do such buildings offer as part of our built environment and why should they be preserved?

TEST YOURSELF AT my-etest.com

CHAPTER 21
URBAN GROWTH AND THE ENVIRONMENT

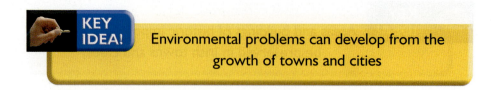

KEY IDEA! Environmental problems can develop from the growth of towns and cities

As world population grows, more and more people are living in towns and cities. Urban growth on a large scale began with the Industrial Revolution in 1750 when coal was first burnt in engines to produce steam for power. Today, the combustion of fossil fuels, peat, coal, oil and natural gas in cities for heating, transport, industry and power is releasing huge amounts of **carbon dioxide, chlorine** and **nitrous** and **sulphur oxides** into the atmosphere. These gases create major environmental problems for urban and rural areas.

THE GREENHOUSE EFFECT AND GLOBAL WARMING

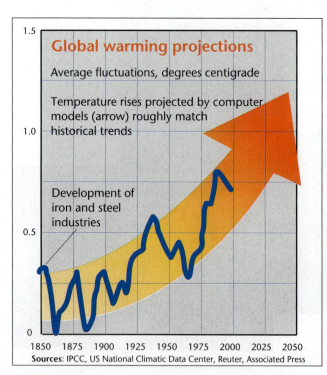

Fig. 21.1 *How have global temperatures been affected by the iron and steel industries? Use evidence from the chart to support your answer.*

Industry and people's homes and their cars produce vast quantities of greenhouse gases. These greenhouse gases will allow the sun's rays through but will not allow heat radiated from the earth's surface into outer space. As these gases increase in the atmosphere so too does the amount of heat from the earth. This build-up of heat is causing the earth's atmosphere to overheat, leading to global warming. This is expected in time to lead to a corresponding rise in sea levels and submergence of some coastal areas.

The United States, an urbanised society, contains just 5 per cent of the world's population but produces 25 per cent of the gases that cause global warming. Approximately 7 tonnes of greenhouse gases are emitted per person every year in the USA and these gases increased by about 3.8 per cent between 1990 and 2000. About 82 per cent are from burning fossil fuels to generate electricity and to power cars. As an individual, you can affect 32 per cent of the total emissions per person, by choices you make in three areas of your life. These areas are the **amount of electricity** we use in our homes, the **waste** we produce and the **type of personal transportation** we use.

URBAN GROWTH AND THE ENVIRONMENT

Class activity

Carefully study the chart in Figure 21.2 showing the per capita (per person) production of greenhouse gases by the world's most developed countries.
1. Which country has the greatest per capita production of greenhouse gases?
2. How does Ireland rank in this table?
3. How does Ireland's per capita production compare with all other European countries?
4. What changes in our lifestyle should we make to reduce this production level?

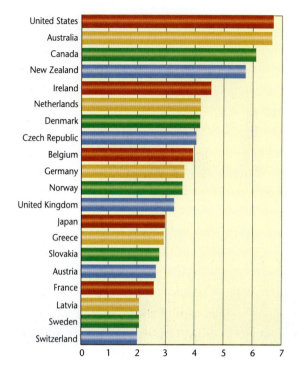

Fig. 21.2 Greenhouse gas emissions per capita MMTCE/million people

Smog

Smog is a combination of smoke and fog. The word accurately describes the canopy of air pollution that hangs over a densely built-up area in winter under calm atmospheric conditions. This is when there is an **air inversion**, with cooler, still air near ground level trapped by warmer air above. And because there is no wind to blow it away, the smoke belching out of chimneys and car exhausts builds up in the air.

Smoke is the most visible pollutant; but it may conceal a range of dangerous chemicals, such as sulphur dioxide and nitrous oxides as well as a variety of gases from industrial plants. Above a certain level of concentration, smog causes a deterioration in health, especially among those already suffering from respiratory complaints, such as asthma or bronchitis. Old people, young children and those who already have lung disease are the most vulnerable.

Explain MMTCE/million people

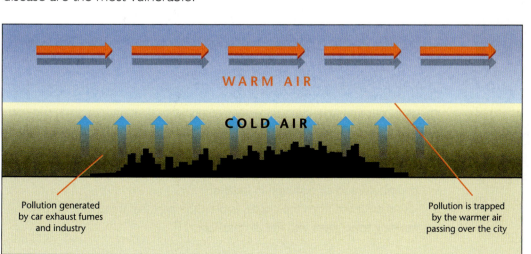

Fig. 21.3 Air inversion

URBAN PROBLEMS AND PLANNING STRATEGIES

Los Angeles regurlarly suffers from severe smog conditions

When toxic gases accumulate in the air over large cities, such as Los Angeles or New York, they form a brownish-pink layer of polluted air. Smog allows only a hazy sunshine through most of the time. It can be so dense that visibility may at times be limited to only a few hundred metres. Smog irritates the eyes and throat and may cause respiratory failure in times of extreme pollution. It also corrodes building materials over a relatively short time.

Class activity
1. What is smog?
2. How does smog affect the urban environment?
3. How does smog affect people's health?

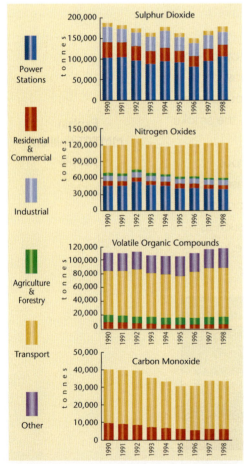

Fig. 21.4 Transport in Ireland contributed 50 per cent of all nitrogen oxide, 60 per cent of volatile organic compounds and 81 per cent of carbon monoxide in 1998

Case Study: Environmental Protection Agency report for Ireland 2000

This report indicated that it will be difficult to achieve in the foreseeable future the standards of air quality demanded by the European Union, especially in Dublin's city centre. The pollutants causing the greatest concern are tiny particles of smoke and gases such as nitrogen oxide. Both of these pollutants come mainly from traffic fumes. The **highest levels of pollution** in Ireland are found in Dublin's city centre and are higher than the limits set by the EU. In addition, the highest pollution levels occur along the main traffic routes and areas of greatest traffic congestion. The times of **greatest pollution coincide with traffic rush hour** in the morning and evening. In places where traffic congestion has been improved a noticeable drop in pollution levels has also occurred.

Class activity
Carefully study the charts indicating sources of greenhouse gases in Ireland.
1. Identify the greatest producer of each of the following gases: carbon monoxide; nitrogen oxide; volatile organic compounds; sulphur dioxide.
2. What evidence in these charts shows that urban areas are major contributors to air pollution in Ireland?
3. Using evidence from the charts, explain the part that transport plays in emitting toxic gases into the atmosphere.

Ireland has signed various **international agreements**, called **protocols**, to reduce emissions of greenhouse gases and ozone-damaging chlorine over the period 1990–2010. Ireland's 'Environmental Millennium Report' states that there were no substantial reductions in air pollutants in Ireland during the 1990s. For many years, Ireland has generated one of the highest per capita emissions of some gases, such as sulphur dioxide. The outlook in relation to greenhouse gases is of much more concern as **emissions in 2010 will be at least 30 per cent higher than in 1990** if present trends continue. This projected increase is more than twice that allowed by Ireland's legally binding commitments under the **Kyoto Protocol** of 1997. One of the reasons for this difficulty is that the Irish economy is highly fossil fuel intensive.

> The ESB coal-fired power station at Moneypoint in County Clare is introducing new methods to reduce sulphur emissions.

URBAN WASTE

Almost 30 per cent of urban sewage waste in Ireland goes untreated into inland rivers and lakes and into coastal waters. One of the most pressing problems is the increase in waste generated in the Greater Dublin area. Sewage receives no treatment or only preliminary treatment prior to discharge in 53 (36 per cent) of the 390 urban areas studied by the Department of the Environment in 2000. A further 38 per cent receives only primary treatment, 21 per cent secondary treatment, and only 5 per cent has nutrient reduction treatment. However, some urban areas, including Dublin and Galway, are building new treatment facilities. Over one billion euro is being invested under the National Development Plan 2000–2006 for wastewater treatment.

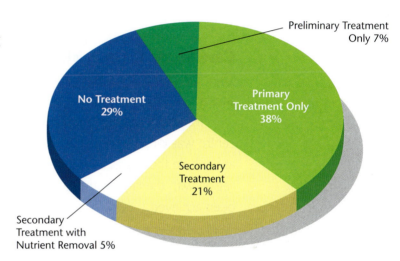

Fig. 21.5 Sewage treatment facilities for urban areas. Carefully study the chart and use evidence from it to: (a) give two reasons for large-scale pollution in Ireland's rivers and lakes; (b) outline one way of reducing this pollution.

The Environmental Protection Agency's Millennium Report found that sampling programmes for soil testing are mostly non-existent in local authorities and few have implemented new management systems.

Class activity
1. What are international protocols?
2. Find out which industrialised nations withdrew from the Kyoto Protocol.
3. Explain (a) the political reasons for this withdrawal; (b) the effects on world pollution levels.
4. The location of refuse dumps has become a major social and political issue in Ireland in recent years.
   (a) Explain where refuse dumps are generally located.
   (b) Explain why these locations cause controversy with (i) locals; (ii) environmentalists/conservationists.

CHAPTER 22
URBAN PLANNING AND URBAN RENEWAL IN IRISH CITIES

KEY IDEA! How effective are urban planning and urban renewal in solving urban problems in Irish cities?

SOLVING TRAFFIC PROBLEMS IN SOME IRISH CITIES

Case Study 1: Limerick City

Over the past 30 years Limerick Corporation's Strategic Development Plan has recorded substantial achievements in a number of areas.

Transport management. Because the development of Limerick City as a regional centre was directly connected to the industrial development of the surrounding region as a whole there was a need to integrate the transportation needs of the developing region with the city. A strategic transport plan was prepared and the following aims have been achieved.

Shannon Bridge over the River Shannon

- Two new bridges have been built in the city: the Shannon Bridge and the Abbey Bridge. The second new bridge, the Abbey Bridge, is part of a new northern ring road that connects the Ennis and Dublin roads. Some old derelict parts of Thomondgate on St Mary's Island were demolished to make way for this development.
- Childers Road, a ring road, has been completed.
- Five new multi-storey car parks have been built in the city centre for off-street parking.
- A disc parking system was introduced to improve traffic flow by restricting parking times to one or two hours.
- Some new pedestrian crossing points have been created as well as improved traffic light systems for pedestrians.
- Proposals are in place for new cycle paths within the city.

Because congestion is still a major problem in Limerick City a new phase of ring road development is in progress. This new development will create an outer ring road that will bypass the entire city, **cross the River Shannon** and link all major routes to Dublin, Tipperary/Waterford, Cork, Kerry, Foynes and Ennis/Shannon/Galway.

Class activity: Route Options

Consultants have studied several different options for crossing the River Shannon in terms of their effect on many issues including the environment, traffic in Limerick City, national traffic, shipping, safety and cost.

Two possible options for crossing the River Shannon were proposed: a low-level opening bridge; and a tunnel.

Low-Level Opening Bridge
Advantages
- Less environmental impact on River Shannon during construction.
- Potential for pedestrian and cyclist use.
- Potential for extra traffic capacity with hard shoulders.
- Less expensive to construct than tunnel.

Disadvantages
- Delays to traffic when bridge is open.
- Risk of ship collision.
- Risk of mechanical failure, which would cause disruption to road traffic and/or river traffic.
- Impact on River Shannon during construction.
- Cost/maintenance.

Tunnel
Advantages
- Neutral visual impact on surrounding landscape.
- Open 24 hours a day, all year round.
- No impact on shipping or leisure craft.
- No disruption to traffic.

Disadvantages
- More expensive to construct than low-level opening bridge.
- Temporary impact on River Shannon during construction.
- Disposal of large quantities of spoil.
- Cyclists and pedestrians not permitted.
- Cost/maintenance.

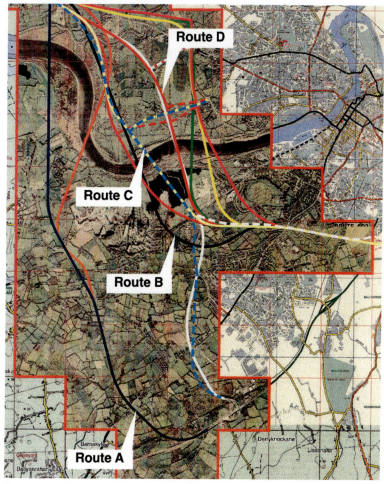

Routes considered

Carefully study the map and information on the previous page and this page.
1. Which in your opinion is the better option: (a) a tunnel; or (b) a low-level bridge? Give three developed reasons for your choice. Use evidence from the map to support your answers.
2. You are now faced with four choices for the bypass route.
   a. Choose one of these (Route A, Route B, Route C or Route D) as your first choice.
   b. Give two reasons why this is the best option.
   c. Which is your least desired route option?
   d. Give two reasons why this route is undesirable.
3. The clear fresh water area in the centre is a potential natural park amenity.
   a. Explain how this resource could be used as part of Limerick's Strategic Plan of the city (see Green Belts and Natural Areas within Cities, pages 113–14).
   b. Explain how route options C and D could interfere with these plans.
   c. How effective do you think this development will be in solving some traffic problems in Limerick? Explain!

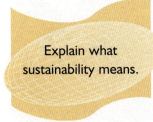

Explain what sustainability means.

Case Study 2: Dublin City

The Greater Dublin area comprises the local authority areas of Dublin Corporation and part of the counties of Kildare, Meath and Wicklow. **The Dublin Transport Office (DTO)** was set up in 1995 to implement the strategic land use planning programme for the Greater Dublin area. This programme is outlined in Figure 22.1. It is based on a 'vision statement' of the city for the future.

Vision statement
- A City and Region which embraces the principles of sustainability.
- A leading European City, proud of its heritage and looking to the future.
- The National Capital, seat of government and national centres of excellence.
- A strong, competitive, dynamic and sustainable region.
- A Living City and Region, on a human scale, accessible to all and providing a good quality of life for its citizens.

One of the most important aspects of this process is the planning for traffic flow up to 2011. The first task of the DTO was to review the work of the Dublin Transport Initiative (DTI) programme introduced in 1995. Its findings showed that growth to date has far outstripped transport projections, caused by the unprecedented level of economic growth of recent years (Celtic Tiger). This growth in transport has been influenced by:
- Rapid economic growth.
- Increase in population.
- Number of households and people at work.
- Growth in car ownership and use.

These factors have created very large increases in levels of traffic, resulting in much greater congestion within the Dublin region. Table 22.1 shows that total morning peak hour trips grew by 78,000 or 45 per cent between 1991 and 1997. However, the bulk of that growth was caused by private car journeys. In 1991 the private car accounted for 64 per cent of peak-hour trips; by 1997, that had increased to 72 per cent. The average journey time by car increased from 31 minutes in 1991 to 43 minutes in 1997, reflecting greater congestion and longer journeys. By 2016, total peak-hour trips are forecast to be 488,000, a 95 per cent increase on the 1997 level.

Table 22.1 Demand for travel (thousand person trips)

	1991	1997	1999	2016
A.M. peak hour	172	250	283	488
Off-peak	107	157	179	256

Class activity
Carefully study Table 22.1.
1. What percentage rise on 1999 figures in morning peak-hour and off-peak-hour travel is expected to occur by 2016?
2. What effects on transport and the social environment will occur within Greater Dublin if Dublin's Strategic Plan is not implemented?

The strategy

The DTO Strategy has two interdependent elements:
- **Demand management**, which seeks to reduce the growth in travel while maintaining economic progress, and which is designed to encourage a transfer of trips, especially at peak periods, from the private car to public transport, cycling and walking.
- **Infrastructure and service improvements**, including a substantial expansion of the public transport network (see below), some strategic road construction and traffic management.

Remember: DTO stands for Dublin Transport Office.

Transport demand management. Dublin's strategic plan includes the following elements, all of which must be implemented if the plan is to succeed.
- An integrated public transport system that can be reached by walking 10 minutes or less and involves no more than one transfer.
- Strategic but limited road improvements.
- Traffic and traffic parking policies that restrict the use of private cars.
- Improvement of freight transport to ports and airports.
- Good quality cycling and pedestrian facilities.
- Complementary and eco-friendly land use policies.

Infrastructure and service improvements. This transport programme includes the following transport facilities.
- Quality Bus Corridors (QBC).
- Dart/suburban rail.
- Luas on-street light rail.
- Metro.
- Park and ride (car parking facilities at suburban rail stations).
- Traffic management and parking programme to reduce private car use.
- Quality cycling routes and cycle parking spaces.

Fig. 22.1 Dublin Transport Office's Strategic Planning Guidelines. To which towns will new routeways be developed in the future?

In addition to Dublin's strategic plan, the **National Roads Authority**, established in 1994, has responsibility for the development and management of our national primary roads. The strategy for these national primary roads is to focus on **four key corridors** and to allocate at least 70 per cent of total expenditure on national primary roads to these corridors. The four strategic corridors are:
- North/South: Belfast-Dublin-Rosslare-Waterford-Cork.
- Southwest: Dublin-Limerick/Shannon and Cork.
- East/West: Dublin-Galway and Sligo.
- Western: Sligo-Galway-Limerick-Waterford-Rosslare.

A large percentage of new road development, such as the bypasses of Waterford and Limerick and the extension to the M50 in Dublin, may be funded by **public-private partnership** (PPP) schemes. These schemes are able to utilise the design and construction **expertise of both public and private bodies** to minimise cost to the taxpayer. These **PPPs may** involve **toll charges** on new developments over a 30-year period to recoup cost and maintenance charges to investors and obtain the best value for money. Through tolling the user pays for the road or bridge facility. Because these toll routes are additions to existing routes drivers can choose to use the existing toll-free routes or the toll routes. Approximately one-third of all existing motorway routes in the EU are toll routes.

Fig. 22.2 Public transport networks in Dublin

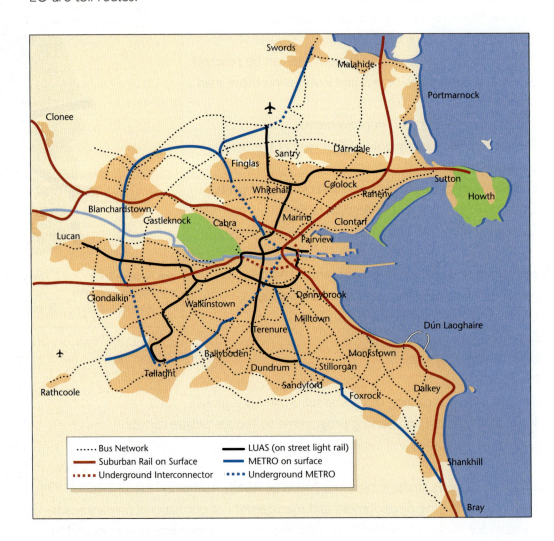

Class activity
1. Use the information in Figure 22.2 to explain the Luas system and its advantages.
2. The Metro system is somewhat similar to Luas except that it will have a higher level of separation from the immediate environment.
   (a) Explain what the difference between the Luas and Metro systems in simple terms.
   (b) How will the Metro system affect congestion within the city?
   (c) Suggest why some parts of the Metro system are to be underground.

URBAN PLANNING AND URBAN RENEWAL IN IRISH CITIES

Class activity

Carefully study the land use distribution maps of Dublin in Figure 22.3.
1. List in rank order the land uses in Dublin in 1956.
2. List in rank order the land uses in Dublin in 2000.
3. Identify Phoenix Park (it is the largest open public space in any EU city). Then, using this as a reference (aid), describe and explain how urban expansion has affected land use distribution in the city.
4. How effective has urban planning since the 1960s been in the protection of green spaces within Dublin? Use evidence from the maps to support your answer.

Green belts can be used for many different social activities that improve the quality of life in urban areas

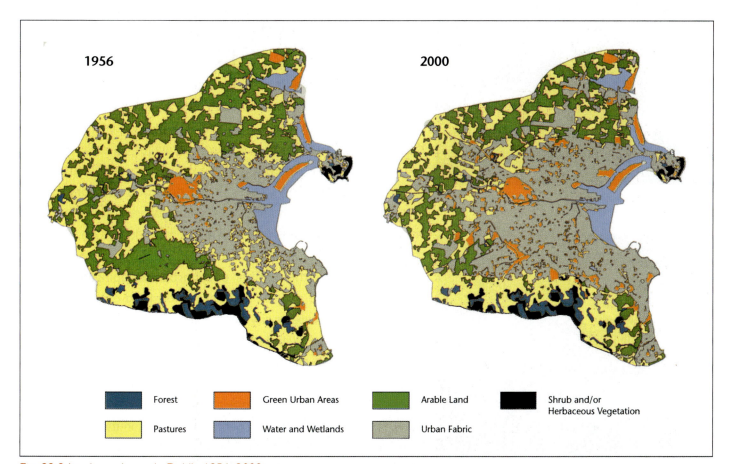

Fig. 22.3 Land use change in Dublin 1956–2000

THE IMPORTANCE OF PROGRAMME REVIEWS IN STRATEGIC PLANS

Planning reviews are important because they may identify new trends or highlight the continuation of older trends. Reviews of Limerick's social programme indicates that:

- There is a disturbing trend of city clubs leaving the inner city and acquiring facilities in more rural areas.
- City clubs have difficulty in getting the necessary finance to improve their present facilities.
- Large areas of land owned by the corporation, which could have been used to retain some of these community facilities within the inner city, lie undeveloped.

Solutions to Findings

The City Corporation intends to sell off some of these lands to raise money for investment in community facilities. Planning and planning reviews therefore indicate that finance can be raised and money can be invested in those facilities that need finance through the planning process. This measure may reduce migration from the city to the suburbs.

Shopping centres were initially developed in Ireland's cities in the 1970s

RETAILING AND EMPLOYMENT IN THE CITY CENTRE

Retailing is a matter of utmost importance to the growth and development of all cities. In terms of floor area it is a major land user, and gives rise to demands on traffic flow and parking facilities. Retailing is also a major employer, accounting for up to 20 per cent or more of the total employment in a city. The principal attraction of **city centre shopping** is generally the **non-food category**, such as clothing, sports goods and household appliances. Therefore the viability of a city centre is dependent to a great degree on traditional shopping patterns. **So for city centres in Ireland to continue to thrive the number of suburban shopping centres must be restricted and the number of non-food outlets be encouraged to locate in city centre areas only.**

We have already studied the effect of suburban downtowns on large cities such as New York and Los Angeles. Large suburban shopping centres in Ireland act in a similar way to suburban downtowns in America and attract more and more business as they grow larger. The restriction on non-food outlets in these areas will therefore demand that people continue to shop in city centres.

Identify a new hotel, apartment block and shopping centre in this photograph

URBAN RENEWAL PROGRAMMES

Urban renewal programmes are essential to the revitalisation of inner city areas. These programmes have identified obsolete and derelict sites in all Irish large towns and cities. To achieve the goals of strategic urban plans the government introduced new schemes that offered **tax incentives** for the development of these sites for industrial, commercial and residential uses.

These schemes created the movement of money that would otherwise simply have lain unused in bank accounts. These investments created jobs, jobs created income, income created spending and spending demanded products that created additional jobs. In addition the redevelopment of derelict sites in inner city areas brought **new life to city centre** shopping areas. Their new modern shopping facilities and streetscapes and restaurants encouraged people to visit city centre districts by day and at night.

Some areas in Ireland's cities that have benefited from urban renewal programmes include Cruises Street in Limerick, Broad Street in Waterford, Merchants Quay in Cork and Temple Bar in Dublin.

Urban renewal schemes have transformed inner city areas into vibrant and dynamic residential and shopping districts

Class activity
1. Explain why the pattern of shopping within a city must be controlled for a city to remain dynamic.
2. Explain ways that local governments encouraged urban renewal schemes.
3. Explain some advantages of urban renewal schemes in some Irish cities.

CHAPTER 23
EXPANSION AND PROBLEMS IN DEVELOPING WORLD CITIES

KEY IDEA! Problems include:
- Housing
- Basic Services
- Unemployment
- Transport

The pull factors that draw people to cities and have led to the rapid growth of urban areas and urban populations lead to serious problems in providing housing, basic services and jobs. These factors have also created intense congestion in squatter settlements and on the streets of cities in the developing world. In addition, the gulf between the minority rich and majority poor is greater in cities of the developing world than in advanced (rich) societies.

HOUSING PROBLEMS

The flood of rural migrants to cities of the developing world is causing a housing crisis in those cities. Most authorities have failed to provide adequate shelter for their rapidly growing urban populations; and most of the poor must survive by their own efforts and skills. Estimates suggest that one-third of urban dwellers of the developing world cannot find or afford accommodation that meets basic health and safety standards. Consequently they have three options:
- To sleep rough on pavements or other public places.
- To rent a single room if they have some money.
- To build their own shelter on land they do not own and have no legal right to build on.

SHANTY TOWNS

Self-built shelters or 'squatter settlements' are called shanty towns. They are generally located on the outskirts of cities, on small inner city sites or on hillside sites, many of which are unstable and prone to landslides. Shanty dwellers face the constant threat of eviction or the bulldozing of their homes. Nobody knows how many people live in any one shanty. Most figures are estimates. It is estimated that 30 per cent of Rio de Janeiro's total population live in its shanties. The equivalent figures are 25 per cent in Sao Paulo, 45 per cent in Mexico City, 40 per cent in Bombay and 60 per cent in Calcutta.

Homes in shanty towns are generally of a poor standard. Walls may be made from galvanised iron, plastic, or cardboard boxes, while the main frame of the dwelling is often of poles nailed together. Roofs are of similar materials, often stabilised with weights such as old tyres. In some parts of Calcutta, large concrete pipes are used as shelters. Many shanties are built on land that is liable to flooding. In Guayaquil in Ecuador, shanties extend out into the tidal bay. Homes are connected by raised wooden pathways over the water.

In Calcutta, permanent slums or bustees are well protected in law. Residents cannot be ejected and are entitled to basic services, such as water and light. Pavement dwellers, those who literally live on the city's sidewalks or in traditional squatter havens, such as under bridges, along canals, on land destined for roads, or other public use, are not protected and don't receive services. They can be moved when government desires without relocation or compensation. Still, some pavement dweller families have lived on the same spot for three generations.

Over time shanty families renovate and improve their homes. However, some shanty 'houses' are leased to families. They readily evict those bustee families who cannot pay the rent. Many of these 'houses' have just one room no bigger than a standard sized bathroom. A family of eight may occupy such a tiny space that serves as both a kitchen and bedroom. Houses are generally clean and tidy. **One in three people in Calcutta live in bustees** and over 500,000 homeless people live and sleep on the streets.

What conditions evident in this photograph indicate serious housing problems?

> Squatter settlements are not necessarily slums, but many of them are. In Chile squatter settlements are called callampas, mushroom cities: in Turkey they are called gecekondu, meaning they were built after dusk and before dawn. In India they are called bustees; in Peru barriadas; in Brazil favelas and in Argentina simply villas miseries, villages of misery.

BASIC SERVICES

Basic services, such as clean water supplies, rubbish removal and mains sewage disposal, are available only in small areas of some shanties. **Open sewers** are common and the stench of human waste is ever-present. This odour increases when temperatures are high in summer. In south-east Asia monsoon rain causes sewers and canals to overflow. Such contaminated 'warm' water creates an ideal breeding ground for malaria, cholera and typhoid and other water-borne bacteria. Immunisation programmes are inadequate or non-existent and many people die unnecessarily. Over **11 million children under the age of five died in 2000**, most from preventable causes.

The absence of electricity supplies in relatively new shanties severely hinders the improvement of hygiene standards.

In developing countries **one child in three does not complete five years of schooling**. Providing primary education for everyone remains a great challenge. Success in this area will give millions more the skills to rise out of poverty. Enrolment rates are up in most regions, but the quality of education has been suffering. Far too many children remain out of school. To increase enrolments and provide better education, resources

Many children attend makeshift schools in shanties

Great numbers of unemployed poor people line street pavements in Calcutta

(money) must be invested in training teachers and improving facilities. Governments must also **increase family and community participation, and eliminate gender bias** that limits educational opportunities for girls.

Because of declining birth rates, the world's school-age population will increase by only 9 million in the next 15 years. But there are large regional differences. As a consequence of the desire for smaller families in east Asia the school-age population there will decline by 22 million. But in sub-Saharan Africa it will rise by 34 million. Added to the 47 million not now in school, that means building schools, training teachers and providing textbooks for an extra 81 million children in the next 15 years. The many continuing **civil wars in Africa** are denying millions of African children a primary education. Many of these children live in urban slum areas.

UNEMPLOYMENT

The right to work is a basic human need. Without work there is no money for countless millions of shanty dwellers. They do not have access to social welfare benefits. Many shanty dwellers belong to the 'informal sector'; that is, they have to find their own form of employment. They may provide services such as driving rickshaws or work as street traders (selling drinks etc.), shining shoes, or making saleable goods out of waste products. They live at **subsistence level** – making just enough to get by. As a consequence their children suffer from malnutrition because their diet lacks fresh vegetables, protein, calories and vitamins. This has other implications. **Malnutrition** is a symptom of poverty. There are over 150 million underweight children in developing countries, a large percentage of whom live in shanties. Malnutrition inhibits mental and physical development. In addition, malnourished mothers are more likely to have low-weight babies. So the cycle continues.

Often new arrivals to the shanties far outnumber the available jobs, so unemployment is high.

TRANSPORT

Governments in wealthy countries direct vast amounts of money towards reducing traffic congestion in cities. In many cases they are making only slight improvements. In Ireland, for instance, billions of euro are being invested in improving urban traffic, yet many feel that in Dublin we are losing the battle. Our roads and streets are clogged with traffic, especially during rush hour. That this situation has deteriorated so rapidly in recent years in a city with a little over one million people has surprised even the planners.

It is not difficult, therefore, to understand that **congestion** occurs in developing world cities where **populations exceed 10, 15 or 20 million people**, and most figures are only estimates. However, the type of congestion can vary. In India, for example, **local traditional forms of transport**, such as rickshaws, oxcarts, donkeys and, in some cases,

> **Class activity**
> 1. Explain three major social problems affecting urban regions in developing world countries.
> 2. Explain how the lack of one basic social service prevents many shanty dwellers from reaching higher levels of employment.
> 3. Explain how social unrest can lead to low educational standards.

elephants, compete with other road users. Even though the dream of owning a motor car is beyond the wildest dreams of most Indian people, some Indian cities, such as Delhi, are clogged with cars, buses and trucks.

The speed of expansion of cities in developing countries has had a direct effect on traffic flow. This rapid growth is unprecedented anywhere else in the world. Karachi in Pakistan, a city of 1.1 million people in 1950, now has a population of 11 million and is estimated to reach 20.6 million in 2015. Cairo may reach 15 million in 2015 from 2.2 million in 1950. It took London 190 years to grow from half a million to 10 million and New York 140 years to grow by the same extent. By contrast, **Mexico City, Sao Paulo, Rio de Janeiro, Calcutta and Mumbai all took less than 75 years to grow from half a million to 10 million inhabitants each**. In addition, over one-third of all the inhabitants in each of these cities lives in unplanned, overcrowded, mostly un-serviced shanties. Congestion is part and parcel of their character and it is difficult to see any great change in this situation in the foreseeable future.

Congestion is an everyday experience on streets in cities of the developing world

Case Studies: developing world cities in the Indian sub-continent

The Indian sub-continent (also called south Asia) includes such countries as India, Bangladesh, Pakistan, Nepal, Bhutan and Sri Lanka. It is a natural region: an area that has been created by natural forces such as climate, drainage and earth movements. It differs from surrounding regions in its climates, soil types, vegetation and fauna. Some of its major characteristics are:

- It is a clearly defined **natural region**, bounded by mountains, deserts and ocean; the Indian Peninsula is Eurasia's largest.
- It is the world's poorest region, with low incomes, low levels of education, poorly balanced diets and poor overall health.
- With only 3 per cent of the world's land it supports 20 per cent of the world's population (1.036 billion people) and 66 per cent of the world's poorest people. Almost half of its people earn less than the equivalent of US$1 per day.
- Half of its children are malnourished and underweight, most of them girls.
- Its population growth rates are among the highest in the world.
- India is the world's largest democracy.

When people move to cities they tend to have smaller families. Incentives that cause rural couples to have many children do not prevail in the cities, where living space is limited and confined. Urbanisation, therefore, contributes to reduced rates of natural increase in populations.

URBAN PROBLEMS AND PLANNING STRATEGIES

Fig. 23.1 What physical characteristics define the Indian sub-continent as a natural region?

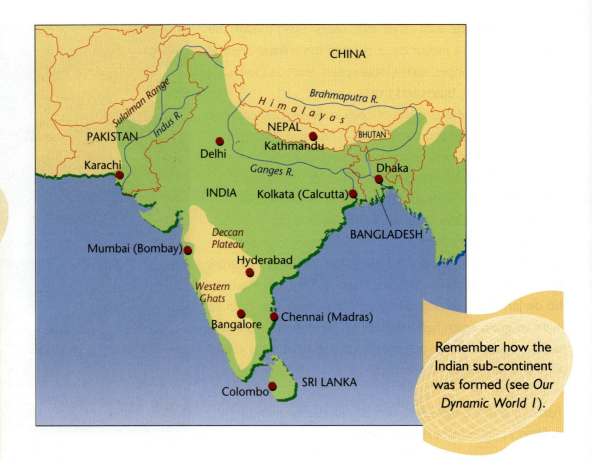

Mountains, deserts and coastlines combine to make the Indian sub-continent one of the world's most vividly defined geographic regions. To the north the Himalayas creates a natural 'wall'. To the east, mountains and dense forests divide the region from south-east Asia. To the west, rugged highlands, the Sulaiman Range, and large deserts separate it from its neighbouring countries Iran and Afghanistan.

Remember how the Indian sub-continent was formed (see *Our Dynamic World 1*).

Draw a map of the Indian sub-continent. Then on the map mark and name the main cities, rivers, deserts and elevated areas.

India is not, as yet, a highly urbanised society. However, we should not lose sight of the numbers involved. Only 26 per cent of its population lived in cities in 2000, but that 26 per cent represented more than 260 million people – nearly as many as the entire population of the United States.

India's rate of urbanisation is on the rise. People are arriving by the hundreds of thousands in the already teeming cities, swelling urban India by about 5 per cent annually, almost three times as fast as the overall population growth. Not only do the cities attract people here as they do everywhere else, many villagers are forced off the land because of widespread poverty in the countryside.

Calcutta (Kolkata), eastern India

Calcutta has a population of 12.7 million people and a natural increase of 2 per cent. The city has 500,000 homeless people and over 4 million of Calcutta's population live in slums called Bustees.

Calcutta was the political capital of Britain's Indian Empire until Delhi was chosen in 1911. Calcutta remained India's largest trading, financial and industrial centre until well into the 1950s, when Bombay became more important. Now there are fewer factories in Calcutta than there were 40 years ago, and fewer jobs in manufacturing. The city's economic decline is indicated by the fact that of all Asian mega-cities, it alone has a minus net migration figure. More people move out than in. 'Poor people in Bihar, a part of Calcutta's hinterland, may travel the width of India to Bombay in search of work rather than go to Calcutta.' (Extract from *A Decent Place to Live – Urban Poor in Asia*.)

Part of Calcutta's problems stem from the political division that created Pakistan and East Pakistan (now Bangladesh), cutting off a large part of **Calcutta's hinterland** and filling the city with **500,000 refugees**. The Indian part of the city had risen virtually without any urban planning, and the migrants created almost unimaginable conditions.

Housing. Calcutta is notorious for its slums and pavement dwellers even though other cities may be as badly off in this regard. For over 20 years international agencies and the government have tried to improve living conditions in the city by supplying water taps and toilets. However, maintenance is usually so bad the end results are little better than at the beginning.

Industry and roads. No new industry has been established in the city for years. As industrial production has declined so has the real income of workers. There have been several development problems for Calcutta and its satellite cities. Nearly all have tried to disperse population by developing industry throughout the metropolitan area. However, it has not worked because the necessary roads and bridges were not finished in time to support the changes. In addition, the city lacked the energy and drive to develop into smaller growth centres that could take root and thrive on their own.

Many women and children work in unsafe environments in Calcutta in order to earn meagre incomes to enable them to survive

The Indian government supports many of Calcutta's industries, but at a high cost. Old industries, such as carpet making and cotton weaving, continue to use child labour to enable them to compete in foreign markets. The hinterland of Calcutta – Bihar – is sometimes called **India's Rustbelt** and it is the poorest of India's 25 states. Part of this decline is due to the poverty of its neighbouring states such as Bangladesh around the Bay of Bengal.

Bombay (Mumbai), western India

Bombay is located on India's western coastline. Western India is experiencing slightly increasing prosperity. It faces the rich Middle East, the Gulf of Iran and the Arabian Peninsula, where many oil-rich states prosper.

Like Calcutta, Bombay is a city of migrants. However, more like London, Paris or New York than Calcutta, Bombay contains many people of so many races and languages, Indian, Middle Eastern and European, that there is no one tongue in general use there. Modern Bombay has one of the highest population densities, about **476 people per hectare**. This is four times that of New York City. It is estimated that **77 per cent of all families have only one room in which to live**. Some rooms are rented out in eight-hour shifts. However, it is not all bad news. Cities like Bombay offer hope.

Bombay is the leading industrial city in the state of **Maharashtra**, the **leading industrial region in India**. Many people from this region have worked in the oil-rich states to the west and either sent money home to their families or, more importantly,

Remember the ethnic, racial and cultural difficulties that face the Indian sub-continent at present.

Bombay is one of India's rapidly industrialising cities. It attracts many back-room service industries for multinational companies.

used their savings to establish small service industries. Maharashtra is an outward-looking region establishing new links with world markets. Many small private industries manufacture goods ranging from umbrellas to satellite dishes and from toys to textiles.

The **prosperity** of this region is **spreading along the Indian coast of the Arabian Sea**. The beaches of Goa to the south and Gujarat to the north are attracting European tourists who favour newer destinations for their holidays.

Class activity

1. Explain how India's natural region formed initially.
2. Identify and describe India's boundaries that define it as a natural region.
3. The cities of India face many difficulties. Use the following headings to explain the severity of these problems: (a) rapid urban growth; (b) unemployment; (c) population density.

CHAPTER 24
THE FUTURE OF URBANISM

ISSUES RELATING TO CITIES OF THE FUTURE

It was once said that 'there are new-born baby towns: doddering old-man towns: fat millionaire towns: quiet studious towns: loud blatant towns: towns with all the luck: towns with no luck at all: dying towns: dead towns and ghost towns. Towns are very human'. This is a somewhat light-hearted description, but one that contains much truth, and the observer had a deeper understanding of the growth and character of towns than his words might suggest. Cities, however, are more complicated. They are complex spaces where webs of technologies, such as water supplies, energy, transport and communication networks, bind spaces together while social, recreational and employment activities keep its various communities apart.

The old concept of western-style cities where 'wealth trickles down' is no longer the reality. Wealth is now confined to certain areas within cities while poverty is confined to areas that house forgotten communities. So it is misleading to speak of 'the city' as if it were a single unit. Cities of today (and of tomorrow) are places:

- Composed of different parts, culturally mixed and multi-centred urban areas.
- Where intense connections exist with far-off places and frightening disconnections between neighbourhoods.
- Where past assumptions that 'far-off people and places may not relate while close-up ones do' are not necessarily true.
- Where stark contradictions and huge tensions co-exist.
- Where highly planned and expensive developments that took planners and skilled consultants many years to put together exist in some areas, while other parts of the same city appear to be uncared for.

Modern cities often display great contrasts in people's income and living conditions

The Dual City

The term 'dual city' relates to social division within urban areas. This is based on evidence of increasing social division (rich versus poor) where a large proportion of a city's population are cut off from the wealth-creating activities, such as services and manufacturing industries, that we normally associate with improving people's quality of life. This group forms what is termed an **'underclass'** and is surplus to the needs of a 'modern' society. This group of poor people is composed of a very high proportion of ethnic minorities, sick, elderly, disabled people and single parents who have become socially isolated from many areas of city life. Inner city areas and council estates have become identified with these minority groups. In addition, within these 'underclass urban

Class activity

1. Explain what is meant by 'the dual city'.
2. Explain, using examples, what the author means by 'This age of extremes is becoming an acceptable social policy'.
3. Explain why increased international migration could lead to increased social division within cities.

areas', **many make a living on an informal basis** (paid in cash, tax-free) or illegally, independent from the taxable income of society in general.

The policy of including the urban poor in a city's development, as was the case in the twentieth century, is being undermined. This new policy, encouraged by recent economic trends such as the Celtic Tiger and by government policy, **leads to exclusion** from the chance or ability to improve one's living standards, and to alienation from the general population. This **'age of extremes'** is becoming an **acceptable social policy** as if it were the inevitable evolution of life within cities of the future everywhere, especially as urban populations increase across the world. This results in a growing sense of **despair among the poor** and an increasing **fear among the rich**. This fear among the rich is reinforced by trends in international migration and the mixing of a wide range of ethnic and racial groups and leads to a severe separation of rich from poor.

This increasing separation or alienation will eventually lead to a situation where the rich or affluent will live and interact only with each other, while the poor will live and interact only with poor people. This trend is encouraged when many people are forced out of the housing market by higher pricing and when social or local government housing is reduced or withdrawn completely. The United Nations reported that between 1995 and 1999 the world's 200 richest people doubled their wealth to more than US$1 billion. At the same time 1.3 billion people continued to live on less than a dollar a day. The 447 richest people in 1996 had a combined wealth in excess of the annual income of the poorer half of the world's richest people.

Urban Renewal, Mega-projects and Flagship Developments

Social improvement of cities is too often related to the physical and economic structure and appearance of cities rather than to the quality of life of its existing citizens.

Derelict urban areas are often cleared to make way for modern flagship developments

Urban renewal projects generally affect local housing in two ways:
1. The physical removal of poorer residents. Physical removal may occur when existing dwellings are demolished to make way for newer developments. The demolished buildings are generally cheaper, low-value dwellings that serve low-income and vulnerable members of society.
2. Forced out-migration through forced house price increases. Rundown hotels and rooming accommodation that provided a valuable source of cheap accommodation are demolished.

Mega-projects. Urban mega-projects represent a new, specialised form of the urban living environment that is being rapidly introduced throughout cities across the globe by a combination of design consultants, investment groups and planning authorities. Such mega-projects include casinos, parks, multi-storey cinemas, hotels, offices, expensive high-security housing (gated communities) and sometimes golf courses with security personnel to ensure safety. The United States has many such developments, for example in Florida. They are also becoming popular in the cities of India, China and south-east Asia but to a lesser degree than in the developed world.

Many mega-projects may be funded through tax incentives and zoning, giving rise to dispersed settlements throughout some cities with no clear planning strategy for their locations.

Flagship developments include office developments such as Canada Tower at Canary Wharf in London's Docklands. (The proposed development for Dublin's dockland area was rejected by planning authorities in 2001 as it was believed to be too large a development for a medium-sized city. They favoured a scaled-down version of the same proposal.) These developments are generally financed through some form of public-private partnership between government and private individuals or companies. Dublin's financial centre (IFSC) is a huge success that has created many jobs and investment companies.

Most cities will try to promote themselves as a good place to live and work. The cities promote their business opportunities as well as their lifestyle activities. Now as always, cities are desperate to create the impression that they lie at the centre of something exciting. Dublin's image abroad as a young, vibrant city with good night life and a yuppie culture may be attributed in part to our numerous rock groups, such as U2.

New apartment blocks have been built in many Irish cities

Dublin's cafes, nightclubs and street furniture create the image of a city confident in itself and its future

Class activity
1. Explain what is meant by (a) mega-projects; (b) flagship developments.
2. Explain why Dublin has become a major tourist centre in recent years.

Canary Wharf was a flagship development in London's docklands

Industry

The image of industry within a city is changing. It is no longer associated with the factory, the smokestack chimney and the storage yard of the nineteenth and twentieth centuries. Now it promotes itself within well-designed landscaped lawns and gardens, lakes and sculptures, such as in Park West in Dublin. Industrial buildings are ultra-modern, futuristic buildings of mirrored glass and high technology. Their industrial activities are no longer the heavy, dirty and dangerous work of the past, but technology, skill and cleanliness.

Mega-projects, flagship developments and new business parks act as economic stimulants or magnets that are intended to attract people, spending and jobs that create a cycle of consumption, products and employment. They may act as stimulants to other economic developments by local authorities or others that aim to spread the effects of development across the city.

The use of Public Space and Social Control

CCTV cameras often help in regulating traffic and identifying thieves

The streets and pedestrian public spaces where people had more or less free and open access are beginning to be used more and more only by '**those who belong**'. The poorer citizens 'stand out' and homeless people are moved on. Urban public space has never been truly public in many countries. Some cities, such as London and Dublin, still have their public spaces, such as Hyde Park and St Stephen's Green.

Surveillance within cities. In many cities, the activities of many people or groups are constantly monitored by **CCTV cameras**. The cameras are sometimes used to exclude poor groups from some areas, such as from high-priced shopping centres in Sao Paulo in Brazil. Thirty 'danger zones' have been identified in Berlin, giving police extensive new powers of search and eviction.

'Undesirables' are excluded from redeveloped areas in many US cities. Some geographers question whether 'public space' still exists in some western cities. Have shopping malls become the controlled public spaces of future cities as middle-income people flock to these centres on Sundays and at festive seasons?

When CCTV was first introduced it was expected that it would lead to:
- A significant reduction in crime within CBD areas, creating a 'feel-good factor' among shoppers and residents.
- A revitalisation of town and city centres through increased consumer use and spending.

However, there has been no properly conducted survey to prove whether or not CCTV leads to crime reduction. Indeed there is the suggestion that the presence of CCTV has led to the feeling that responsibility for security lies elsewhere or that somehow cameras by their very presence enforce security, leading to 'bystander indifference' to crime and disturbances in city centre areas. The use of CCTV won widespread support in Britain and it is now an accepted feature of many towns and cities today.

The Development of Neighbourhoods and Sustainability

It has been argued that long-term successful development of cities in the future lies in **encouraging development at neighbourhood level**. So instead of planners and consultants dictating massive structural change to cities so that they will prosper, the more practical and realistic way forward is for neighbourhoods to deliver solutions to a neighbourhood's own problems with their own resources or with government aid. So the key to sustainable neighbourhood success seems to lie in rejecting blueprints from outside in favour of those generated locally, which build on local expertise and knowledge, respect local conditions, and have social and environmental aims.
This is called **'organic planning'**. It is based on the principle that what works in one neighbourhood is not necessarily likely to work in another.

> **Class activity**
> 1. Explain two ways that CCTV cameras have helped improve social order in Irish urban areas.
> 2. Explain one way that CCTV cameras may be viewed as a negative development within urban areas.
> 3. Explain what is meant by the statement 'The success of an urban region depends on development at neighbourhood level'.

Picture Credits

For permission to reproduce photographs and other material, the author and publisher gratefully acknowledge the following:

PHOTOS:

ALAMY IMAGES: 3 B, 21, 24, 25 B, 37 T R, 44 C, 105 T © Alamy Images

ANTHONY BLAKE PHOTO LIBRARY: 37 T L © Maximilian Stock Ltd; 94 © Gerrit Buntrock

PETER BARROW PHOTOGRAPHY: 75, 103, 109 B, 110 B, 113 © Peter Barrow Photography

CAMERA PRESS IRELAND: 50 T, 61 L, 123, 129 T, 153 © Camera Press Ireland

COLLECTIONS: 59 B © Jill Swainson; 76 T R, 115 L © Geray Sweeney; 76 B R © Will Moody; 79 B, 132 B L © Michael Diggin; 89 © Marc Schlossman, 90 © Alain Le Garsmeur; 114, 115 R © Michael St Maur Sheil; 132 B R © Avril O'Reilly

CORBIS: 1 T R © Gallo Images; 1 B R © Tom Wagner/Corbis Saba; 3 T, 147 T © Paul A. Souders; 7 © Owen Franken; 9 © Guy Stubbs/Gallo Images; 12, 151 © Earl & Nazima Kowall; 18 © Jennie Woodcock/Reflections Photolibrary; 25 T L © Bill Stormont; 28, 46, 50 B R, 56, 117 B © David Turnley; 30 © Lindsay Hebberd; 31 © Stephanie Maze; 32 T © Rob Lewine; 32 B © Brian A. Vikander; 33 T © Andrea Jemolo; 33 B © Michael S. Yamashita; 34 T © Dallas & John Heaton; 35 B © Tiziana and Gianni Baldizzone; 37 B, 38 © Howard Davies; 45 T and B © Jose Luis Pelaez Inc; 50 B L © Robert Patrick/Corbis Sygma; 53 © Cochrane James/Corbis Sygma; 54 © Bettmann; 57 T © Steve Raymer; 57 B © Richard T. Nowitz; 58, 136 © Nik Wheeler; 60 T © Paul Almasy; 63 T R © Joseph Sohm/ChromoSohm Inc; 63 B © David Ball; 70 © Sandro Vannini; 71 C, 100 C, 108, 143 © Michael St. Maur Sheil; 71 B, 86 © Yann Arthus-Bertrand; 74, 100 B, 101, 132 T © Richard Cummins; 85 B R © Alain de Garsmeur; 93 © Geray Sweeney; 100 T © Alan MacWeeney; 109 T © Felix Zaska; 110 T © Robert Essel NYC; 112 © Carl & Ann Purcell; 116 B L © Tim Page; 117 T R © WildCountry; 121 B © Gian Berto Vanni; 122 © Charles E. Rotkin; 125 © David Zimmerman; 128 T © Lester Lefkowitz; 131 B © Craig Aurness; 148 © Reinhard Eisele; 149 © Dean Francis/Corbis Sygma; 155 B © London Aerial Photo Library

ESLER CRAWFORD PHOTOGRAPHY: 78, 87 © Esler Crawford Photography

KEVIN DWYER: 62/65, 77 T, 144 B © Kevin Dwyer

DEPT OF THE ENVIRONMENT, HERITAGE AND LOCAL GOVERNMENT: 76 T L © Dept of the Environment, Heritage and Local Government

IRISH IMAGE COLLECTION: 44 B, 61 R, 69, 71 T, 73, 76 B L, 77 B, 81, 82, 85 T, 85 C, 95, 116 B R, 116 T, 117 T L, 121 T, 127, 128 B, 129 B, 130, 131 T L, 131 T R, 138, 144 T, 154, 155 T, 155 C, 156 © Irish Image Collection

IRISH PICTURE LIBRARY: 44 T © Irish Picture Library

ORDNANCE SURVEY: 67, 79 T, 120, 126 © Ordnance Survey

PANOS: 1 B L, 152 © Mark Henley; 35 T © Giacomo Pirozzi; 118 © Crispin Hughes; 119 B © Martin Adler

PHOTOCALL IRELAND: 47, 119 C, 119 T, 145 © Photocall Ireland

PHOTO IMAGES LTD: 49, 60 B, 85 B L, 88 © Photo Images

REX FEATURES: 29 B © Sipa Press; 39 © Great Percy; 63 T L © Andy Drysdale

SCIENCE PHOTO LIBRARY: 19 © John Cole; 22 © Joseph Nettis

STILL PICTURES: 25 T R, 34 B, 105 B © Mark Edwards; 29 T © Gil Moti; 147 B © Hartmut Schwarzbach

NEIL WARNER PHOTOGRAPHY: 92 L, 92 R © Neil Warner, www.warnerphoto.org

OTHER PHOTOS: courtesy of the author (83); courtesy of Park West Property Marketing (105 C)

MAPS:

92 T courtesy of Galway County Council; 106 courtesy of Galway City Council. Other maps are reproduced by permission of the Ordnance Survey of Ireland.

T = top, B = bottom, C = centre, L = left, R = right

The author and publishers have made every effort to trace all copyright holders, but if any has been inadvertently overlooked we would be pleased to make the necessary arrangements at the first opportunity.